Exploring Options in Academic Writing

EFFECTIVE VOCABULARY AND GRAMMAR USE

Jan Frodesen
University of California, Santa Barbara

Margi Wald
University of California, Berkeley

Ann Arbor
University of Michigan Press

ISBN-13: 978-0-472-03426-0

2019   4   3

Acknowledgments

We want to thank those who have provided useful insights as we planned the many classes and conference presentations that have built the foundation for this book. Jan would like to thank her colleagues in the English for Multilingual Students Program at the University of California, Santa Barbara, especially Judy Gough and Roberta Gilman, for their interest in this project. Margi would like to thank her colleagues in the College Writing Programs and Summer English Language Studies Program at the University of California, Berkeley, many of whom have sampled early versions of our work. We also thank our students, who continually push themselves to become stronger writers and in turn have pushed us to learn more about their needs as academic writers and ways in which we could help them meet those needs.

Perhaps our biggest thanks go to Gena Bennett and Diane Schmitt, with whom we have collaborated on TESOL grammar and vocabulary colloquia and who have given us support in so many ways throughout the very long process of making this book a reality. And we thank all of the instructors who have attended our presentations, contributing to this book through their feedback and encouraging us to share our practices with an even larger audience. We thank our anonymous reviewers for helpful suggestions on our work in progress.

For support and encouragement during the years of this book's development, Margi would like to thank Mark Roberge and Alice Savage, and Jan would like to thank Mike Rose, the Winbigler-Hendershot family (Nancy, Jim, and Ted), and Phyllis and George Brown.

Finally, no set of acknowledgments would be complete without expressing our deep appreciation for the undying support, feedback, and patience of our editor, Kelly Sippell. She gave us the time, space, and freedom to create the kind of textbook we wanted. For this we are grateful. Her contributions to this book and to the field of TESL and academic English publishing are immeasurable.

Grateful acknowledgment is made to the following authors, publishers, and individuals for permission to reprint previously published materials.

Mark Davies and *the Corpus of Contemporary American English (COCA): 450 million words, 1990–present* for content in Figure 1.4: Inside the Corpus of Contemporary American English (COCA); in Figure 1.5: Frequency Results for *accordance* in COCA; in Figure 1.6: Context Results for *accordance* in COCA; and in Figure 1.8: Context Results for *dwindled* in COCA." Used with permission. Available at http://corpus.byu.edu/coca/.

Oxford University Press for content from *Oxford Advanced Learner's Dictionary (online): permeate* and *interrogate,* copyright © 2015. Available at www.oxfordlearnersdictionaries.com/us/definition/english.

Oxford University Press for content from *Oxford Collocations Dictionary for Students of English:* adjective + *evidence,* copyright © 2009.

Every effort has been made to contact the copyright holders for permission to reprint borrowed material. We regret any oversights that may have occurred and will rectify them in future printings of this book.

Contents

Introduction

Exploring Options in Academic Writing is designed to help student writers develop their knowledge and use of academic language to meet demands of college- and university-level writing assignments. It draws on the research identifying lexical and grammatical patterns across academic contexts and provides authentic reading contexts for structured vocabulary learning. Recognizing that vocabulary choices in writing often require consideration of grammatical structure, ***Exploring Options*** focuses on specific kinds of lexico-grammatical decisions—that is, ones involving the interaction of vocabulary and grammar—that student writers face in shaping, connecting, and restructuring their ideas. It also helps writers learn how to effectively use resources such as learner dictionaries and concordancers to develop their academic word knowledge.

Rather than being structured as a series of academic word lists or selected grammatical features that students need to master, this book integrates instruction in vocabulary and grammar by considering the goals that all writers must pay attention to in producing effective academic discourse. Such goals include choosing words that "fit" their writing contexts not only in meaning (semantically), but also in relationship to the grammar of phrases or clauses and in the level of formality required; they also involve showing relationships between ideas within sentences, creating connections across sentence boundaries through a variety of appropriate cohesive devices, expressing writer stance, or referencing source materials accurately and effectively.

To assist students in achieving these goals, each chapter of ***Exploring Options in Academic Writing*** provides scaffolded instruction that will help students check their current lexico-grammatical knowledge and build on that knowledge by using available resources and engaging in guided text analysis and production tasks.

Exploring Options has these specific objectives:

1. to make students aware of paper and online resources for developing academic language proficiency and ways to use these resources effectively

2. to provide guided practice in strategies for crafting lexico-grammatical structures needed for academic writing

3. to familiarize students with vocabulary used for particular academic discourse functions, such as showing relationships between ideas, expressing stance, focusing information, and creating cohesion.

Recent research reveals the complexity of academic language learning and the need to integrate grammar and vocabulary in language instruction. The activities in this book are based on a synthesis of current research that responds to two overarching questions:

What Do Students Need to Know about a Word to Use It Correctly in Their Writing?

The development of active vocabulary involves more than the mere knowledge of a word's meaning. Writers have to control the use of a word in their writing: denotations, connotations, collocations, grammatical characteristics/context, register/level of formality, frequency of use, and word forms/derivatives (Nation, 2001).

What Types of Language Structures Are Used Most Frequently in Academic Writing?

Much of this book examines the ways in which the choice of vocabulary drives the use of grammar. Corpus linguistics in particular, which identifies how language is used across registers and genres, has produced a wealth of new information about lexico-grammatical patterns (Biber, 2006; Biber et al., 1999; Hinkel, 2002) and is now available through dictionaries, concordancers, and other resources. Corpus and functional linguistics analyses also highlight common grammatical features of academic writing that differ from those used in spoken contexts and thus, we believe, should form the focus of academic writing courses. Some features that tend to be used with high frequency in academic writing that are practiced in this text are:

- complex sentence structures
- noun phrases, nominalizations, abstract nouns, and signaling or classifier nouns, such as *the <u>development</u> of written <u>work</u> appropriate for university assignments*
- cohesive devices, as in these phrases: *<u>given</u> these criteria* and *<u>despite</u> such requirements*
- hedging devices to express stance, as in this sentence: *Students <u>tend to</u> / <u>often</u> rely on the language characteristics of speech.*

Structure within Chapters

Following the introductory chapter of ***Exploring Options,*** most of the chapters include two sections: Raising Language Awareness and Building Your Knowledge.

Raising Language Awareness

This section provides an introduction to features of the target structures or writing subskills and gives students opportunities to identify their current level of exposure and understanding.

Building Your Knowledge

This section, the main part of each chapter, offers explanations about various aspects of the targeted vocabulary or structure that seem most relevant and challenging for student writers. These features have been selected partly on the basis of observations on how the targeted vocabulary is used in academic writing, including analysis of vocabulary in corpus-based resources. We have also selected them drawing from our experience working with students and their texts.

Numerous guided activities in this section help students gain awareness of the range of lexico-grammatical options and develop strategies for implementing them effectively in their own writing. Expanding on what it means to know a word as outlined and explained in Chapter 1, the explanations and activities in Building Your Knowledge offer exposure to many aspects of vocabulary knowledge that go beyond just knowing word meanings.

The activities in Building Your Knowledge represent a range of complexity and types, including **text analysis, practice selecting and using structures in authentic and constructed texts,** and **error analysis and editing practice.**

References

Biber, D. (2006). *University language: A corpus-based study of spoken and written registers.* Amsterdam: John Benjamins.

Biber, D., S. Johansson, G. Leech, S. Conrad, & E. Finegan. (1999). *The Longman grammar of spoken and written English.* London: Longman.

Hinkel, E. (2002). *Second language writers' text: Linguistic and rhetorical features.* Mahwah, NJ: Lawrence Erlbaum.

Nation, I. S. P. (2001). *Learning vocabulary in another language.* Cambridge, U.K.: Cambridge University Press.

Chapter 1: Using Resources for Vocabulary Development

Many students note that vocabulary is the one thing they need most to be successful academic writers: They want to learn more words and how and when to use them. And students often complain about receiving the following marks in the margin of their papers: word choice (**wc**), wrong word (**ww**), or awkward (**awk**). Unfortunately, it is quite hard for a student to know how to address these types of problems: If the student had known the correct or better word to use, most probably, he or she would have used it!

We all have what researchers call **receptive vocabulary** (words that we recognize and understand when we read them) and **productive vocabulary** (words that we understand, that we know how to use accurately, and that we can pull from our memories when we are writing). In order for us to be able to use and remember a new word, research suggests that we need to come in contact with that word many times. Also, each word has a set of characteristics that writers need to know—not just its meaning but also the rules for its use—in order to use the word correctly in a sentence. In this book, you will be working with vocabulary frequently used in academic writing, some of which you already use in your writing and some of which you may not use yet. This chapter aims to give students the tools (strategies, resources, and knowledge) to help them investigate the characteristics of academic vocabulary they are less familiar with in order to use words correctly in writing and in order to tackle comments like **wc, ww,** or **awk** when they receive them on their papers. The subsequent chapters offer practice with common academic words and phrases so that students can not only use them accurately but also be able to access them when they write.

1.1 CHARACTERISTICS OF A WORD

This section introduces the types of word characteristics that you need to know in order to use a word correctly in a sentence: **denotation** (a word's meanings), **literal vs. figurative meanings, connotation** (the feeling a word creates), **register** (a word's level of formality), **frequency of use in different contexts, collocations** (other words that are often used with a word), **spelling, derivatives** (word forms), and **grammatical environment** (the structures that come before or after a word).

Exercise 1

Part 1. Each pair of sentences highlights the first two characteristics of a word that help writers know how to use a word correctly in a sentence: denotation and literal vs. figurative meanings. Each pair of sentences contains the same word used in different ways. For each pair, explain the difference in meaning between the two underlined words.

1. a. The researchers <u>counted</u> the number of responses given by each participant.

   b. How much do student evaluations <u>count</u> in the reviews of instructors?

   _____

   _____

2. a. During the practice trial, the Olympic athlete set a new record in the 110-meter <u>hurdle</u> race.

   b. Coming from a very low-income background, he faced many financial <u>hurdles</u> in college.

   _____

   _____

Part 2. Each pair of sentences highlights three more characteristics of a word that help writers know how to use a word correctly in a sentence: connotation, register, and frequency of use in different contexts. Each pair of sentences contains close synonyms that cannot be used interchangeably because they have different characteristics. For each pair, explain the difference in characteristics between the two underlined words. Use a dictionary as needed.

3. a. After the plane crash, the investigators <u>interviewed</u> the pilots.

   b. After the plane crash, the investigators <u>interrogated</u> the pilots.

   _____

   _____

4. a. Researchers compiled <u>tons</u> of evidence to support their position.

   b. Researchers compiled <u>abundant</u> evidence to support their position.

   _____

   _____

5. a. Scholars dismiss this theory as <u>risible</u>.

   b. Scholars dismiss this theory as <u>ridiculous</u>.

   _____

   _____

Table 1.1 summarizes the characteristics of the words highlighted in Exercise 1.

Table 1.1: Characteristics of a Word, Part I

Type	Examples	Notes
Denotation	a. The researchers <u>counted</u> the number of responses given by each participant. b. How much do student evaluations <u>count</u> in the reviews of instructors?	It is important to understand the different meanings a single word might have. In this case, in the first example, *count* means "to calculate the total number of something," whereas in the second sentence, it means "to have value or importance."
Literal vs. figurative meanings	a. During the practice trial, the Olympic athlete set a new record in the 110-meter <u>hurdle</u> race. b. Coming from a very low-income background, he faced many financial <u>hurdles</u> in college.	Many words can be used in different contexts to create different shades of meaning. In this case, the first example concerns a more literal, physical context: a race in which runners jump over hurdles. In the second, the hurdles are not literal or physical. They are abstract or figurative.
Connotation	a. After the plane crash, the investigators <u>interviewed</u> the pilots. b. After the plane crash, the investigators <u>interrogated</u> the pilots.	A word's connotation refers to how strong of a feeling the word creates. It is possible that either verb accurately describes the situation with the pilots. For example, the second sentence is much stronger in feeling, suggesting that the investigators might feel that the pilots had done something wrong.
Register	a. Researchers compiled <u>tons</u> of evidence to support their position. b. Researchers compiled <u>abundant</u> evidence to support their position.	Register refers to the style of language, grammar, and words used for particular situations. In the first sentence, we see a shift in register: the content is for academic writing and requires a more formal word choice than the word *tons*.
Frequency	a. Scholars dismiss this theory as <u>risible</u>. b. Scholars dismiss this theory as <u>ridiculous</u>.	*Risible* is used very infrequently in English. There is not necessarily anything wrong with using a less-frequent word, like *risible*, in the correct context, especially if the meaning is checked. However, one danger of simply choosing a word out of a thesaurus is not knowing how frequently the word is used and perhaps overusing it.

Exercise 2

Read the sentences, each of which might receive one of these comments: **wc, ww, awk**. Underline the words, phrases, or clauses that you think sound awkward or may contain an error based on the clue given at the end of each sentence. The hints in parentheses after each sentence refer to one of the characteristics of a word that dictates how to use the word correctly in a sentence. If possible, list how you might change the sentence to address this concern.

1. Researchers are quite interested about the relationship between socioeconomic status and acquisition of academic English. (*Hint: Consider the prepositions.*)

   _____

   _____

   _____

2. In her article, Santos sites several studies that examine this relationship. (*Hint: Consider spelling/homophones.*)

   _____

   _____

   _____

3. According to these researchers, unequal school funding can negatively effect students' success. (*Hint: Consider spelling/word forms.*)

_____

_____

_____

4. It is also important to recognition the debates about bilingual education in the U.S. (*Hint: Consider word forms.*)

_____

_____

_____

5. Many people claim that bilingual education causes that learners develop English skills more slowly than English-only programs, whereas others believe the opposite. (*Hint: Consider grammatical environment.*)

_____

_____

_____

Table 1.2 summarizes the characteristics of the words highlighted in Exercise 2.

Table 1.2: Characteristics of a Word, Part II

Type	Examples	Notes
Collocation	Researchers are quite interested ~~about~~ <u>in</u> the relationship between socioeconomic status and acquisition of academic English.	*Collocation* refers to a combination of words that are commonly used together. If your team wins a close match, you might call it a *narrow victory*, but you would not call the opposite a *wide victory*. You could, however, write that your team won *by a wide margin*. There are not necessarily rules for which words can or cannot go together, so you'll need to investigate words to learn more. In this case, *interested* is followed by *in*, not *about*.
Spelling/ homophones	In her article, Santos ~~sites~~ <u>cites</u> several studies that examine this relationship.	Many words are often confused because, while they are spelled differently, they sound the same. The ones that often appear in grammar handbooks are *there* and *their*, which play very different roles grammatically. In the example, the writer confused *sites* (a noun referring to a location) and *cites* (the verb form of *citation*).
Word forms or derivatives	According to these researchers, unequal school funding can negatively ~~effect~~ <u>affect</u> students' success. It is also important to ~~recognition~~ <u>recognize</u> the debates about bilingual education in the U.S.	In the first example, the writer confused *affect* (the verb form) and *effect* (the noun form). The same is true in the second example. *Recognition* is the noun form; *recognize* is the verb form.
Grammatical environment	Many people claim that bilingual education ~~causes that learners develop~~ <u>causes learners to develop</u> English skills more slowly than English-only programs, whereas others believe the opposite.	Certain words require certain grammatical environments. In this case, the verb *cause* can be followed by a noun (*cause* + a problem) or an object and infinitive (*cause learners to develop*), <u>not</u> a *that*-clause (*causes that learners develop*). Placing a word in the wrong grammatical environment often leads to the **awk** comment in the margin.

Exercise 3

In each sentence, the underlined word or phrase has been used inappropriately. Each sentence has been marked for a particular characteristic of the word from Tables 1.1 and 1.2. Edit each sentence by writing corrections above the underlined words or phrases. The first one has been done for you as an example.

Undoubtedly/Without a doubt
1. ~~Indubitably~~, the current law will save people thousands of dollars. (*frequency*)

2. This bill is now over 60 days past <u>do</u>. (*homophone*)

3. All food has been prepared <u>on</u> accordance with strict safety guidelines. (*collocation*)

4. It is important to conduct a complete inspection annually to ensure that all requirements have been <u>done</u>. (*collocation*)

5. After the incident, the main character in the novel became much more aggressive and <u>violence</u>. (*word form / derivative*)

6. My college advisor suggested <u>me to take</u> another math class. (*grammatical environment*)

There is quite a bit that you have to know about a word—beyond one core meaning—in order to use it correctly in writing. No wonder students who are experimenting with academic vocabulary get so many comments in the margin of their papers! There are, however, a number of resources you can use to help you investigate the aspects of words.

1.2 RESOURCE: LEARNER DICTIONARIES

How many times have you looked up a word in an English-English dictionary only to be more confused by the words in the definition than you were by the word you were looking up? And how many times did you become frustrated when the definition referred to the word itself in the definition (like *having reference* in a definition for the word *referential*)?

Learner dictionaries are different. They may not contain as many words as a large English-English dictionary, but they present more understandable definitions and also show many of the characteristics of a word: derivatives, connotations, collocations, register or formality, and grammatical environment.

Many learner dictionaries are **corpus-based.** A *corpus* refers to a collection of language. To create a corpus dictionary for academic English, the authors compile a large set of language—textbooks; journal articles; transcripts of lectures, discussion groups, and office hour dialogues; and more. They use software to search through the collection to see how a word is really used in authentic situations, what different meanings it has, how common it is, and what grammatical environments it is used in. Because most learner dictionaries are corpus-based, they can present a great deal of valuable information about a word's meaning and use.

Let's start by looking at this sample sentence to see how much information a learner dictionary presents:

Increased activities by drug cartels permeated violence in the community.

Look at Figure 1.1 to see if you can uncover what is wrong with the use of the word *permeate*.

Figure 1.1: *permeate* (from the *Oxford Advanced Learner's Dictionary* online)

permeate *verb*

(*formal*)

1 [transitive, intransitive] (*of a liquid, gas, etc.*) to spread to every part of an object or a place

▶   **permeate something**

◆ *The smell of leather permeated the room.*
◆ *The air was permeated with the odor of burning rubber.*

▶   **+ adverb/preposition**

◆ *rainwater permeating through the ground*

2 [transitive, intransitive] (*of an idea, an influence, a feeling, etc.*) to affect every part of something

▶   **permeate something**

◆ *a belief that permeates all levels of society*
◆ *A feeling of unease permeates the novel.*

▶   **+ adverb/preposition**

◆ *Dissatisfaction among the managers soon permeated down to*
◆ *members of the workforce.*

▶   **permeation**

◆ *noun* [uncountable] (*formal*)

What We Learn:

- **Derivatives:** The entry lists two word forms: (1) the verb form and (2) the noun form, which is uncountable, or non-count. Non-count nouns are always singular, and we do not use words with them that suggest a number (*a/an, several, many,* etc.)

- **Literal vs. figurative meaning:** The dictionary entry provides both the physical or literal meaning (definition #1) and the figurative meaning (definition #2) of the verb.

- **Grammatical environment:** The dictionary entry highlights important information required to use this word appropriately:

  - The verb can be transitive, which means that it is followed directly by an object (*permeated <u>the room</u>*).

  - Or it can be intransitive, which means it is not always followed directly by a noun. In this case, it is often followed by a preposition + noun (*permeating <u>through</u> the ground*).

  - The examples show that the order of words in the sample sentence (see top of page 10) is not appropriate. Each example shows that the item that moves throughout, physically or figuratively, is always in the subject position before the verb in the active voice. The violence is spreading, so the sentence should read: *Violence permeated the community (given the increase in drug cartel activity).*

- **Register:** The entry describes the word as formal.

- **Collocations:** The entry provides information about the kinds of nouns that collocate with *permeate* (an idea, influence, feeling).

Now, let's look up *interrogate* from Table 1.1 (see Figure 1.2).

Figure 1.2: *interrogate* (from the *Oxford Advanced Learner's Dictionary* online)

interrogate *verb*

1 interrogate somebody

to ask somebody a lot of questions over a long period of time, especially in an aggressive way

◆ *He was interrogated by the police for over 12 hours.*

▶ **interrogation**

noun [uncountable, countable]

◆ *He confessed after four days **under interrogation**.*

◆ *She hated her parents' endless interrogations about where she'd been.*

▶ **interrogator**

noun

◆ *His interrogators finally forced him to confess.*

PATTERNS

■ an **in-depth** interview/consultation

■ a **police** interview/interrogation

■ to **have/request** a(n) interview/audience/consultation **with** someone

■ to **give/grant** someone a(n) interview/audience/consultation

■ to **carry out/conduct** an interview/interrogation

Exercise 4

Using the sample entry for *interrogate* in Figure 1.2, complete the exercise based on what you learn.

1. Connotation: What words in the definition tell you the connotation of the word?

2. Derivatives: List the two derivatives or additional word forms given for *interrogate*.

   a.

   b.

3. Countability: The definition lists *interrogation* as both countable and uncountable. Nouns that can be countable and uncountable are often referred to as double nouns. Look at these two examples. In which is *interrogation* countable and in which is it uncountable? What signals the difference?

   a. Amnesty International continues to investigate how people may be mistreated while under interrogation.

   b. The organization has uncovered evidence to show that, in one military prison, suspects have been mistreated in more than ten interrogations.

4. Collocations: Read the sample sentences and examples in the Patterns box. For each sentence, choose a word that fits.

   a. The police decided to _____ an interrogation of the suspect, given the new evidence uncovered the night before.

   b. The suspect was _____ interrogation for over eight hours.

1.3 RESOURCE: COLLOCATIONS DICTIONARIES

Corpus-based learner dictionaries often give some information about common collocations—words that tend to appear together in academic writing. A different kind of dictionary, called a **collocations dictionary,** presents only this information. To create this kind of dictionary, a researcher searches through a corpus for a particular word and then compiles the words that go together with that word most often. Writers can use collocations dictionaries to help them when they are drafting and are struggling to find a word. Writers can also use these dictionaries when they are editing papers and have received comments from instructors. Remember the earlier example in Exercise 1, *abundant evidence?* What other adjectives might go with the word *evidence?* See Figure 1.3.

What We Learn:

- There are many collocations with *evidence.*

- The first seven (before the | line) all focus on the quantity of evidence.

- Each set between the vertical lines contains words that can describe *evidence* in different ways.

- *Tons of evidence* is not a common collocation, confirming the answer in Exercise 1.

Figure 1.3: adjective + *evidence* **(from** *Oxford Collocations Dictionary***)**

ADJ.
  **abundant, ample, considerable, extensive, plentiful, substantial, widespread |
  growing | clear, compelling, conclusive, irrefutable, overwhelming, persuasive,
  positive, powerful, solid, striking, strong, unambiguous, unequivocal
  | insufficient, scant | concrete, direct, firm, first-hand, objective, tangible**
    - convincing, decisive, good, hard, incontrovertible, adequate | flimsy, inadequate
    The figures provide concrete evidence of the bank's claim to provide the best service.

Exercise 5

Several sentences using the word *evidence* are given, each marked by an instructor as having some sort of word use problem. Using the collocations dictionary entry (Figure 1.3), find two possible ways to edit the underlined parts.

                          awkward/register

1. The author presents <u>really great evidence</u> to support his position.

   I believe this evidence makes his argument very persuasive.

                          register

2. Providing <u>only a little bit of evidence</u>, the author fails to

   convince his audience.

3. Much research on the link between athletic participation and

   leadership has been performed on U.S. college campuses,

            word choice

   providing <u>big evidence</u> that student athletes gain strong

   leadership skills.

4. Before this new set of economic data, experts believed that the

   crisis was over. Now, the tables and charts in this report provide

    word choice

   <u>real evidence</u> to support this belief.

Exercise 6

Review Exercise 3. The problem in Item 4 was that the noun *requirements* does not collocate with the word *done*. Look up the word *requirements* in a collocations dictionary or in some online learner dictionaries. List three verbs that are common collocations with *requirement*.

1. _____

2. _____

3. _____

Exercise 7

Each sentence contains a collocation error in the underlined phrase. Using a learner or collocations dictionary, change the wording to correct the error. More than one answer is possible. The first one has been done for you as an example.

1. A good manager is always ready, no matter what <u>situations</u>
   arise
   <u>~~happen~~</u>.

2. The politician <u>did a serious mistake</u> when he used a racial slur in his comment to the press.

3. The Prime Minister noted that the new incentives should <u>excite the economy</u>.

4. The Federal Reserve lowered interest rates, hoping to <u>demise the downward trend</u> in consumer spending and employment rates.

5. Engineers are working on materials that will improve the concrete design of <u>high</u> buildings.

6. <u>From the author's opinion</u>, the proposed policy will not be effective in solving the current political crisis.

1.4 RESOURCE: ONLINE CONCORDANCERS

An **online concordancer** allows writers to search a corpus to see how many times a word is used and in which contexts. While you can get a lot of this information from learner and collocations dictionaries, not all words appear in these sources and the information about collocations and grammatical environments can be limited. A concordancer can provide many more examples of the word in context. Finally, a concordancer allows you to look up phrases, not just individual words. First, let's investigate the word *accordance* (see Item 3 in Exercise 3) in a concordancer. Figure 1.4 shows what an online concordancer looks like.

Figure 1.4: Inside the Corpus of Contemporary American English (COCA)

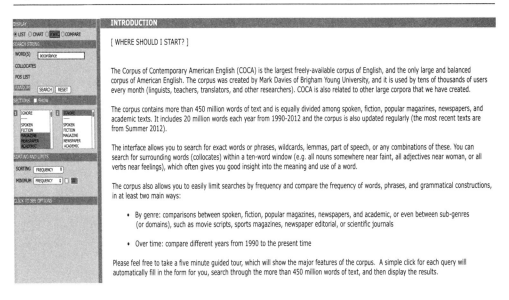

Used with permission.

Figure 1.5: Frequency Results for *accordance* in COCA

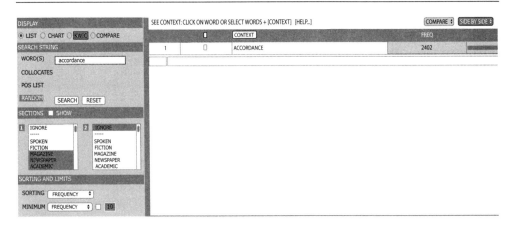

Used with permission.

As shown in Figure 1.5, the word *accordance* appears 2,402 times in the three types of texts (magazine, newspaper, and academic) searched.

Figure 1.6: Context Results for *accordance* in COCA

CLICK FOR MORE CONTEXT			(SAVE LIST) CHOOSE LIST (--------) CREATE NEW LIST ( ) **[?]**	
1	2012	MAG	National Geographic	buffalo, are enacting a primordial, immutable ritual. Both species are behaving in **accordance** with their genetic code. Lions have been hunting African buffalo, and African buffalo
2	2012	NEWS	NYTimes	that the demand for SES exceeds the level of funding reserved for SES, in **accordance** with Title I, Part A, priority will be given to the lowest-achieving students
3	2012	NEWS	NYTimes	up with a letter seeking assurances that " all transfers' were done " in **accordance** with applicable rules and regulations,' according to a copy of the letter.
4	2012	NEWS	Houston	17-page response to questions about its spending, declaring the amounts " reasonable and in **accordance** with industry standards. " # In response to each question by the Chronicle about
5	2012	NEWS	WashPost	the Pentagon to decrease its projected spending by $487 billion over the next decade in **accordance** with a deficit-reduction deal President Obama reached with Congress in August. # Those cuts
6	2012	NEWS	Denver	Pine Ridge from illegal whiskey-sellers. # " Either the federal government shuts Whiteclay down in **accordance** with our treaties with them or we shut them down ourselves as a nation,
8	2012	NEWS	CSMonitor (1)	" The military justice system is fair, and most American warriors act in **accordance** with laws of war, " says Sulmasy, author of The National Security Court
9	2012	NEWS	CSMonitor	be properly dealt with. " Whoever has broken the law will be handled in **accordance** with law and will not be tolerated, no matter who is involved, "
10	2012	ACAD	PracticeNurse	the daily routine. These might include relaxation techniques. # Diet should be in **accordance** with the government's' The balance of good health' advice.14 Other specific diet
11	2012	ACAD	EnvironmentalHealth	North Carolina-Chapel Hill (UNC) and the UAE University Faculty of Medicine. In **accordance** with the cultural guidelines recommended by our collaborators at UAE University, written informed consent
12	2012	ACAD	EnvironmentalHealth	after introducing the quadratic term was statistically significant (p < 0.001). In **accordance**, no pattern was evident in the logistic regression models of high bilirubin (Table
13	2012	ACAD	AmJPubHealth	. # Several specific SNPs were independently associated with mortality in our analysis. In **accordance** with the literature, each additional copy of the APOE? 4 allele increased mortality
14	2012	ACAD	AmJPubHealth	, Goff DC Jr. Deteriorating dietary habits among adults with hypertension: DASH dietary **accordance**, NHANES 1988-1994 and 1999-2004. Arch Intern Med. 2008; 168(3):308-314. # 31
15	2012	ACAD	LibraryResources	about ETDs. 3 # The goal of the integrated system, developed at UNS in **accordance** with CERIF, DC, ETD-MS, and OAIPMH, is to avoid or reduce
16	2012	ACAD	LibraryResources	are available to anonymous users via the Internet. Moreover, the system is in **accordance** with the CERIF standard and meets requirements prescribed by the Republic of Serbia Ministry of

Used with permission.

Clicking on the word *accordance* or the number of occurrences shows the search term's use in context. The first 16 occurrences are listed in Figure 1.6.

The search has provided compelling evidence to support choosing *in* instead of *on* for Item 3 in Exercise 3.

Figure 1.7: Frequency Results for *risible, ridiculous,* and *ludicrous* in COCA

We searched for each of these words in the Corpus of Contemporary American English, which contains more than 450 million words.

Results:

risible: 62 times

ridiculous: 7,906 times

ludicrous: 1,428 times

Next let's look at frequency. In Exercise 1, *ridiculous* and *risible* were shown as synonyms. However, suppose you want to use a word that is more formal-sounding than *ridiculous* and suppose you find *risible* in the thesaurus. Should you use it? See Figure 1.7.

The infrequency of *risible* should make you stop, think, and investigate. Might there be a more frequent synonymous word? How exactly is this word used and in which contexts? Again, it might be fine to use this word once but not several times in one paper.

Exercise 8

Go to an online concordancer and look up each word and its frequency.

Word	Frequency	Word	Frequency	Word	Frequency
indubitably		get		spread	
undoubtedly		acquire		permeate	
without a doubt*		obtain			

*You can search for a phrase, not just a single word, in the Corpus of Contemporary English. Just type the phrase directly into the WORD(S) field.

Aside from telling how frequently a word is used and what prepositions might go with it, the results from a concordancer search can tell us a great deal about the grammatical environment of a word.

This sentence contains an error in the grammatical environment used with the verb *dwindled*.

The high cost of tuition dwindled <u>the student's savings</u>.
(Grammatical environment)

The results for a search of *dwindled* in the COCA concordancer are shown in Figure 1.8. How do the samples from the concordancer compare with the example sentence? Notice in the COCA results

Figure 1.8: Context Results for *dwindled* in COCA

MAG	MotherJones	64 percent of newborn American males were cut. By 2006, that <u>number</u> had **dwindled** to 56 percent. Immigration trends may be partially responsible for the drop-off: Worldwide
MAG	Redbook	've been married for 18 years, and my <u>connection</u> to my husband has slowly **dwindled** down to nothing. I'd always been hopeful that things could get better,
MAG	Astronomy	majority of the houses there feature personal observatories. As the available <u>land</u> at ASV **dwindled**, Turner began acquiring land across the state line in New Mexico. His second
MAG	CountryLiving	the final nail into Sharon Springs' coffin. By 1960, the <u>population</u> had **dwindled** to about 350 residents. Cut to 2008, when Brent Ridge, a physician-turned-brand
MAG	MilitaryHistory	the disaster of the Battle of the Masts and as their <u>holdings</u> in western Europe **dwindled**, they chiefly concentrated on defending the Aegean. In 904, Leo of Tripoli
MAG	ScienceNews	today a densely forested, frigid swath of northern Europe. Forest <u>plants and animals</u> **dwindled** during ancient winters, the scientists say. Crucially, though, geological analyses indicate
NEWS	Houston	during the same period totaling $107 billion, records show. U.S. Coast Guard <u>spending</u> **dwindled** from $7 million in 1992 to just $600,000 last year. # Two other agencies
NEWS	Denver	for Rockies spring games in Tucson has been unimpressive for 18 years, and <u>crowds</u> **dwindled** even as the Rockies became a World Series participant. The numbers were down 6
NEWS	SanFranChron	the San Francisco police drug lab was in crisis. # Its overwhelmed <u>staff</u> had **dwindled** to two technicians, down from six just a few months before - and one
NEWS	NYTimes	over 1.7 billion yen in debt. The attractions fell into disrepair. Tourist <u>numbers</u> **dwindled**. # Now, the town of 7,000 is desperate to attract new visitors.
NEWS	Denver	symptomatic sabbatical issue - this nationally constituted system is one in which <u>public funds</u> have **dwindled**. # In short, it's not the big bad English professor who cheats
NEWS	Denver	private insurance products once covered religious nonmedical health care institutions, but the <u>number</u> has **dwindled** to a handful, Boettiger said. # " What we want, " Jones
NEWS	Denver	to protect the environment in the face of virulent industry <u>opposition</u> that now has largely **dwindled**. # He engineered many incentives for solar- and wind-energy development, and successfully pushed
ACAD	Bioscience	from very recent times. In 2000, the San Miguel <u>population</u> of island fox **dwindled** to only 15 animals, and all of them were removed from the wild and
ACAD	Bioscience	(a species absent from San Miguel) boomed as the local <u>population</u> of foxes **dwindled**. All this demonstrates the fox's powerful role in structuring island ecosystems. Other

Used with permission.

that the item that gets smaller (*number, connection, land, population,* etc.) comes **before** the verb, acting as the subject. In the example sentence, the item that gets smaller (*the student's savings*) comes **after** the verb, acting as the object. We can now revise the example sentence to fit the grammatical environment shown in COCA.

> The student's savings dwindled because of the high cost of tuition.

Another useful function of a concordancer is the ability to search for phrases, not just single words like in a dictionary. Here are two possible ways to get information about the use of phrases:

1. If we search for the phrase *in the other hand*—a phrase many students use to show contrast—we find only 22 instances in the newspaper, magazine, and academic texts in COCA. All but two relate to physical references, like what someone is holding in one hand versus in the other hand.

2. If we search for *on the other hand* in the corpus, we get almost 14,000 results. While not all may be used as part of the contrast connector, the first 50 results clearly show that the correct contrast connector form is *on the other hand.*

Exercise 9

Look up these phrases in COCA. List the frequency of each phrase.

1. in spite of # _____

2. despite of # _____

3. despite # _____

What do the COCA results tell you about the use of these terms?

Part 1 : Showing Relationships within Sentences

Chapter 2: Writing about Increases and Decreases

Whether you are writing in the field of Mathematics, Economics, Physics, Political Science, Education, or some other area, you undoubtedly use verbs and nouns that express the ways in which things increase and decrease. Writers often need to express increases and decreases when describing conditions, processes, reasons, and results—very common functions in academic writing. In this chapter, you will be introduced to and practice vocabulary and structures to express these types of changes.

2.1 VERBS EXPRESSING INCREASES AND DECREASES

Raising Language Awareness

Exercise 1

The verbs in Table 2.1 express ways in which things can increase or decrease. Put a + in the blank next to all of the verbs in the list whose meanings you are familiar with and that you use in your own writing. Put a √ next to those words whose meanings you are familiar with but that you only rarely use. Put a − in the blank next to words you are less familiar with.

Table 2.1: Change-of-State Verbs

___ abate	___ drop (off)	___ peak
___ accelerate	___ dwindle	___ plummet
___ accumulate	___ ease	___ plunge
___ add	___ enlarge	___ proliferate
___ amplify	___ escalate	___ propagate
___ augment	___ exhaust	___ raise
___ boom	___ expand	___ rise
___ build up	___ extend	___ reduce
___ climb	___ fall (off)	___ shoot up
___ compress	___ gain	___ shrink
___ condense	___ grow	___ shrivel
___ contract	___ heighten	___ sink
___ cut	___ inflate	___ skyrocket
___ decelerate	___ intensify	___ slash
___ decline	___ lessen	___ soar
___ deflate	___ lose	___ spike
___ degenerate	___ lower	___ spread
___ deplete	___ maximize	___ swell
___ depreciate	___ minimize	___ subside
___ diminish	___ mount	___ subtract
___ dip	___ multiply	___ surge
___ downsize	___ mushroom	___ tank

Building Your Knowledge

As Table 2.1 shows, many verbs can be used to express increases and decreases—and that list is only a partial one! As you choose the appropriate verb for a context, you may need to consider some of these semantic (meaning) and grammatical features:

1. What kind of increase or decrease do I want to describe? Consider:

   - a number or amount of something

     The population has <u>multiplied</u> nearly tenfold.

     The school district had to <u>cut</u> courses in many of its programs.

   - the ways in which something increases or decreases in physical size

     Firefighters fought the blaze, which had <u>expanded</u> to nearly 5 acres.

     Radiation treatments successfully <u>shrank</u> the tumor.

   - an increase or decrease in importance, value, or overall quality of something

     The website's popularity <u>soared</u> after it was redesigned.

     SUV vehicles have <u>depreciated</u> faster than was anticipated.

   - the degree of intensity in the force or strength of something

     Concerns <u>mounted</u> as the hurricane winds grew closer.

     The crisis <u>eased</u> when the water level behind the dam was lowered.

   - a directional movement: upward or downward (higher or lower)

     As soon as the speaker finished, a hand <u>shot up</u> in the audience.

     The stock market <u>plunged</u> for a second day, dropping 12 percent.

   - an increase or decrease in rate of something faster or slower

     Green painted bike lanes have <u>proliferated</u> in Manhattan's streets.

     The space shuttle <u>decelerated</u> from 17,000 miles per hour when in orbit to a landing speed of 215 miles an hour.

2. Within each of these categories, how big or small is the increase or decrease? For example, does something get a great deal larger, smaller, higher, or lower?

3. How quickly or slowly does an increase or decrease occur? For example, does something happen rapidly, gradually, or slowly?

4. Which verbs can be used to show how someone or something causes another thing to increase or decrease?

5. Which verbs are used in contexts where what increases or decreases is the subject of the sentence?

The strategies and exercises that follow will help you make appropriate choices among the many options by examining the different meanings and uses of these verbs and the words that can modify them.

Using Verbs to Express Changes in Amount, Size, Quality, and Intensity

A large set of verbs can express increases or decreases regarding changes in the categories of number/amount, size, value or quality, and intensity. See Exercise 2 on page 28.

Exercise 2

Decide whether each verb expresses an increase or decrease. Then write it in a box under the correct column in the chart. The first one has been done for you. Two boxes will be empty.

abate	degenerate	gain	mushroom
accumulate	deplete	heighten	proliferate
amplify	depreciate	inflate	propagate
augment	diminish	intensify	reduce
boom	dwindle	lessen	shrink
build (up)	ease	lose	shrivel
compress	enlarge	maximize	spread
condense	escalate	minimize	swell
contract	exhaust	mount	subtract
cut	expand	multiply	subside
deflate	extend		

Verbs Expressing Increase		Verbs Expressing Decrease	
		abate	

Using Transitive and Intransitive Verbs Appropriately

An important part of learning the meanings of verbs is knowing which verbs **can** be followed by a direct object **(transitive verbs)**, which **cannot** be followed by an object **(intransitive verbs)**, and which could be either depending on the context. This is especially true of the verbs expressing increases and decreases. Often for change-of-state verbs, the transitive verb expresses the idea of **making** something larger or smaller in some way, while the intransitive verb expresses the idea of **becoming** larger/smaller (see Table 2.2).

As shown, in many cases an object that is made smaller or larger (*a bag, chances, efforts, concerns*) can often be used as a subject with the same verb to mean "become smaller or larger." However, this is not true with all verbs and nouns that tend to be used together. For example, we may say that someone *condensed information*, but we would not say *information condensed*. Checking a concordancer to see which forms are used can be very helpful.

Table 2.2: Examples of Change-of-State Verbs

Verb	Common Transitive Meaning	Common Intransitive Meaning
condense	to make smaller in size: *I condensed the plastic bag.*	to become smaller: *The plastic bag condensed.*
diminish	to make something less: *This may diminish our chances.*	to become less: *Our chances diminished with each passing day.*
intensify	to make stronger: *We intensified our efforts.*	to become stronger: *Our efforts intensified.*
multiply	to make larger in number: *The huge expenses multiplied their concerns.*	to become larger in number: *Their concerns multiplied.*

Exercise 3

Keeping in mind that some verbs can be either transitive (verb + direct object) or intransitive (verb − direct object) depending on the context, for each pair of sentences, identify the underlined verbs as transitive (T) or intransitive (I). Write the corresponding letter in the blank provided. If the verb is used transitively, circle the object. The first one has been done for you as an example.

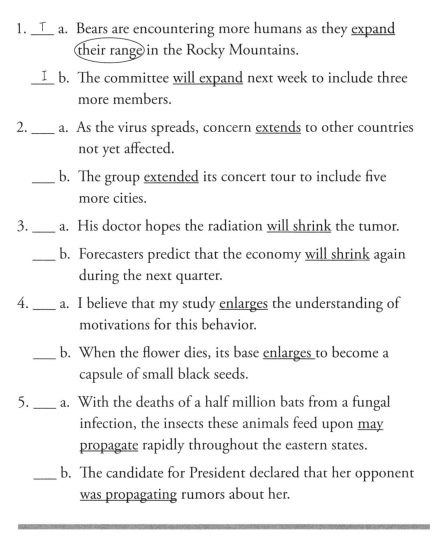

1. _T_ a. Bears are encountering more humans as they <u>expand</u> (their range) in the Rocky Mountains.

    _I_ b. The committee <u>will expand</u> next week to include three more members.

2. ___ a. As the virus spreads, concern <u>extends</u> to other countries not yet affected.

    ___ b. The group <u>extended</u> its concert tour to include five more cities.

3. ___ a. His doctor hopes the radiation <u>will shrink</u> the tumor.

    ___ b. Forecasters predict that the economy <u>will shrink</u> again during the next quarter.

4. ___ a. I believe that my study <u>enlarges</u> the understanding of motivations for this behavior.

    ___ b. When the flower dies, its base <u>enlarges </u>to become a capsule of small black seeds.

5. ___ a. With the deaths of a half million bats from a fungal infection, the insects these animals feed upon <u>may propagate</u> rapidly throughout the eastern states.

    ___ b. The candidate for President declared that her opponent <u>was propagating</u> rumors about her.

One excellent way of building your productive vocabulary is to become more familiar with the object nouns that commonly follow transitive verbs with the meaning of making something larger or smaller.

Exercise 4

Using an online concordancer (e.g., COCA) or a collocations dictionary, find five nouns that can follow each verb as objects. List them next to the verb. If you use a concordancer, check past tense verbs too since they are often more common. If possible, find nouns that are used repeatedly. The first one has been done for you as an example.

Verb	Nouns That Can Follow as Objects
amplify	effects, message, signals, sound, voices
augment	
deplete	
escalate	
lessen	
reduce	

Some verbs are always or often used intransitively—that is, they describe things that become or grow larger or smaller without mentioning who or what causes the action.

Exercise 5

Using a concordancer or collocations dictionary, find four or five nouns that can occur as subjects for each verb. Keep in mind that you may find more concordancer examples with the past tense of the verbs, such as *subsided*, than when they are in the present tense. The first one has been done for you as an example.

Nouns That Can Precede as Subjects	Verbs
symptoms, worries, violence, turmoil, problems	*abate*
	condense
	depreciate
	dwindle
	proliferate
	spread
	subside

Exercise 6

Underline the main verb in each sentence. If the sentence correctly uses a transitive verb, write C in the blank provided. If the sentence incorrectly uses an object after an intransitive verb, write I. Rephrase the sentence using the object as the subject of your new sentence. The first one has been done for you as an example.

_I_ 1. Thousands of newly arrived immigrants <u>boomed</u> the population. _The population boomed when thousands of new immigrants arrived._

____ 2. He dwindled his job opportunities by dropping out of school.

_____

_____

____ 3. Herbs should augment a sound diet and not replace it.

_____

_____

____ 4. The opening of the new oil refinery mushroomed the number of jobs. _____

_____

____ 5. Several aspirin and some rest subsided her bad headache.

_____

_____

____ 6. Plants growing in shade can build up too much nitrogen. _____

_____

____7. The economic recession has shriveled individual savings.

_____

_____

____8. Our company downsized its corporate headquarters last year.

_____

_____

Exercise 7

Using a dictionary or concordancer, identify which one of the three verbs given for each sentence best collocates with the underlined nouns and other underlined words.

1. After days of intense winds and rain, the <u>storm</u> finally _____ .

    a. abated   b. deflated   c. reduced

2. The counseling staff wants to _____ <u>awareness</u> of depression among college students.

    a. accumulate   b. inflate   c. heighten

3. As the semester went on, with every B grade on a quiz, Michael's <u>hopes</u> of getting an A in his computer science course _____.

    a. contracted   b. dwindled   c. reduced

4. I'm sorry to say that it appears we have <u>completely</u> _____ <u>the resources</u> for dealing with this problem.

    a. deflated   b. exhausted   c. lessened

5. The engineers needed to _____ <u>the sound</u> in the auditorium so that those in the back of the hall could hear.

    a. amplify   b. enlarge   c. multiply

6. <u>Tensions</u> _____ as the police refused to let the protesters cross the street.

    a. extended   b. gained   c. mounted

7. <u>The tense situation</u> _____ when one of the protesters fell and was injured.

    a. accumulated   b. escalated   c. expanded

8. However, <u>tensions in the crowd</u> finally _____ as orders were given by the police chief to let the protesters continue with their march.

    a. degenerated   b. depleted   c. eased

Using Verbs to Describe Graphic Data

Another important group of verbs expressing increase and decrease describes upward and downward movement. Some frequent verbs are listed in Table 2.3. These verbs are often used to summarize graphic data in charts and are especially common in Economics as well as research reports in fields that describe and discuss quantitative changes.

Table 2.3: Verbs That Describe Graphic Data

bottom out	fall (off)	raise	skyrocket
climb	lower	rise	soar
decline	peak	shoot up	spike
dip	plummet	sink	surge
drop (off)	plunge	slash	tank

Exercise 8

Choose verbs from Table 2.3 that are synonyms for each phrase.

1. decrease dramatically

    a. _____ b. _____

    c. _____ d. _____

2. increase sharply

    a. _____ b. _____

    c. _____ d. _____

3. reach a low point

    a. _____

    reach a high point

    b. _____

Exercise 9

For each numbered part of Figure 2.1, write a sentence that represents the increase or decrease expressed on the graph. For each sentence, use one of the verbs in Table 2.3.

Figure 2.1: Growth of Wages by Year, 1997–2008

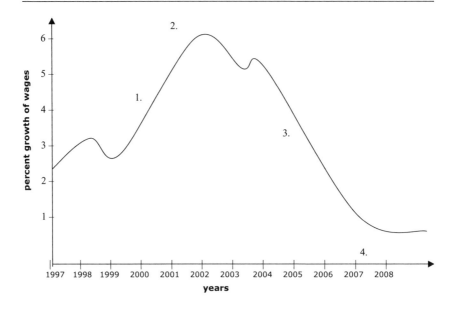

Sentences:

1. _____

   _____

2. _____

   _____

3. _____

   _____

4. _____

   _____

More on Transitive and Intransitive Verbs

As previously noted, it is important to know which verbs can be followed by a direct object (transitive verbs), which cannot be followed by an object (intransitive verbs), and which could be either, depending on the context.

For example, using the verb *proliferate,* we can say *mosquitoes proliferated after the heavy rain*; however, we cannot say *the heavy rain proliferated mosquitoes* because *proliferate* is an intransitive verb and cannot be followed by the direct object *mosquitoes*. (To express the idea in this second sentence, we would need an expression such as *caused mosquitoes to proliferate*.) Many verbs can be either transitive or intransitive, as illustrated in these sentences using the verb *downsize*:

The governor <u>downsized the state's prison population</u> as ordered by the Supreme Court. (transitive)

My parents <u>downsized</u> into a smaller home. (intransitive)

Exercise 10 focuses on this distinction for verbs that can describe graphic data.

Exercise 10

In each pair of sentences, the first verb is transitive and uses a graphic data verb followed by a direct object, and the second is intransitive and uses the graphic verb without a direct object. Write OK in the blank next to the sentences that use the correct grammar. Look up each verb in your dictionary to check samples as needed.

___ 1. a. Bad home mortgage practices tanked the stock market, leading to a recession.

___ b. After the stock market tanked, the country experienced an extended recession.

___ 2. a. The Arts Foundation slashed its budget after its proposal for the grant was denied.

___ b. The budget slashed after the Arts Foundation lost its federal funding.

___ 3. a. Sewage tank malfunctions spiked bacteria levels downstream from the plant.

___ b. After the sewage tank malfunctions, bacteria levels spiked downstream from the plant.

___ 4. a. If the severe drought continues, grocery stores may skyrocket the prices of farm produce.

___ b. If the severe drought continues, the prices of farm produce in grocery stores may skyrocket.

2.2 MODIFIERS EXPRESSING INCREASES AND DECREASES

This section examines how to modify certain nouns and verbs in order to describe the speed and degree of change.

Raising Language Awareness

Exercise 11

Each passage about education contains several expressions of increase and/or decrease, each of which has a modifier before a noun or verb. Underline these expressions and be ready to discuss the different examples. The number of expressions in each passage is given in parentheses. The first expression has been underlined for you as an example.

1. Investing more taxpayer funds in education does not necessarily produce even slight student achievement. A recent study for the Center for an Educated Georgia found that per-student spending over the last generation (adjusted for inflation) <u>dramatically increased</u> in Georgia, while at the same time public high school graduation rates fell sharply. This dramatic increase in operational spending led to significant decreases in class sizes, and marked increases in instructional technology and administration. (5)

2. In the late 1950s, the term study abroad was created, and it became recognized as an innovative path to enrich the undergraduate learning experience. Large private and public institutions first became involved in providing overseas opportunities for their students during the 1960s. Study-abroad programs experienced a dramatic increase in number between the early 1960s and mid-1970s. Since then, the number of education abroad programs has been steadily growing. The growing number of programs has provided many personal and professional opportunities to U.S. college students. (3)

3. Dwindling state funding has forced public colleges and universities to drastically cut services while increasing tuition. One possible solution to the problem of rising tuition is for colleges and universities to put more full-time tenured professors in the classroom. Significantly reducing the other requirements on professors—such as research, scholarship, service, and the like—would, in turn, considerably reduce academic costs. (5)

Building Your Knowledge

Modifying Verbs

As we examined earlier, some verbs—like *surge* or *plummet*—can indicate a very large, rapid increase or decrease. Others—like *grow, rise*, or *reduce*—indicate an increase or decrease but not necessarily its size or speed. In order to express more precise changes, writers often modify verbs like *grow* or *reduce* by using adverbs.

Some adverbs that are commonly used with change-of-state verbs to show the speed or degree/size of change are presented in Figure 2.2.

Figure 2.2: Change-of-State Adverbs Expressing Speed and Degree

Speed		Degree	
abruptly	rapidly	considerably	noticeably
constantly	slowly	dramatically	significantly
gently	steadily	enormously	slightly
gradually	suddenly	markedly	somewhat
quickly	swiftly	moderately	substantially
Both			
sharply			
steeply			

Exercise 12

Place each adverb under *speed* in Figure 2.2 in the appropriate column in the chart. Look up any words you may be less familiar with. An example for each column has been provided.

Fast	Slow	Neutral
quickly	slowly	constantly

Exercise 13

Place each adverb under *degree* in Figure 2.2 on a spectrum from most to least change.

A lot ↑	1.
	2.
	3.
	4.
	5.
	6.
	7.
	8.
	9.
A little	10.

Writers use the words in the *degree* section instead of phrases like *a lot* or *a little*, which are used more frequently in speaking.

Exercise 14

Rewrite each sentence and replace the informal phrases that are underlined with more formal language to express the degree of change. Use one of the adverbs in Figure 2.2 in your revision.

1. After the announcement of her engagement to Prince William, Kate Middleton's public exposure increased <u>a lot</u>.

   _____

   _____

2. The stock market average dropped <u>a little bit</u> after the negative report, but many economists remained optimistic.

   _____

   _____

3. Worldwide support for the country decreased <u>a lot</u> because of the government's questionable humanitarian record.

   _____

   _____

4. The company's sales grew <u>only a little but not a whole lot</u>, so management introduced sales incentives for the upcoming quarter.

   _____

   _____

Modifying Nouns That Express Increases or Decreases

The previous section looked at how to express the speed and degree of change-of-state verbs. Using these change-of-state verbs in place of weaker, more informal verbs can help writers create sophisticated sentences with an academic tone.

> Consumers were much more confident after interest rates went up.

> Consumer confidence increased dramatically after interest rates climbed.

We can also indicate a change by using adjectives to describe nouns. Many of these nouns, such as *climb* or *decrease*, have the same form as the verb. In other cases, there is a difference in the form; for example, the noun form of *compress* is *compression*. The same idea expressed as a verb + adverb can often be expressed in the form of an adjective + noun:

> Stocks <u>climbed sharply</u> at the end of the week.

> A <u>sharp climb</u> in stocks occurred at the end of the week.

These adjective + noun forms can also help academic writers achieve a sophisticated academic tone. Thus, sentences in academic writing tend to rely on noun phrases as opposed to subordinate clauses containing subjects and verbs. This technique is frequently used when writers are echoing ideas from previous sentences. The noun forms of change-of-state verbs can help students achieve such links across sentences, as well as add new information.

> Stocks <u>climbed sharply</u> at the end of the week.

> This <u>sharp climb</u> can be attributed to *a significant increase* in investor confidence.

Table 2.4 shows more examples of verb + adverb and adjective + noun pairs.

Table 2.4: Adjectives and Nouns with Verbs Expressing Change

Verb + Adverb	Adjective + Noun
to rise *abruptly*	an *abrupt* rise (in)
to drop *rapidly*	a *rapid* drop (in)
to fall *suddenly*	a *sudden* fall (in)
to decline *gradually*	a *gradual* decline (in)
to inflate *dramatically*	*dramatic* inflation
to grow *moderately*	*moderate* growth (in/of)
to decrease *slightly*	a *slight* decrease (in)

Exercise 15

Using the patterns in Table 2.4, complete the chart with common adjective + noun collocations. Include frequent prepositions that might collocate with the noun. The first one has been done for you as an example.

Verb + Adverb	Adjective + Noun	Verb + Adverb	Adjective + Noun
to expand considerably	*considerable expansion* *(of, in)*	to cut back sharply	
to reduce constantly		to lose significantly	
to change enormously		to decelerate slowly	
to accelerate gently		to increase steadily	
to decline hugely		to incline steeply	
to inflate markedly		to add substantially	
to dip noticeably		to escalate swiftly	
to drop quickly		to spike suddenly	

Exercise 16

Rewrite the sentences by changing the underlined phrase from adjective + noun to verb + adverb. Make any other changes as necessary. The first one has been done for you as an example.

1a. Belfast experienced a sharp increase in ethnic segregation in the 1970s.

1b. Ethnic segregation increased sharply in Belfast in the 1970s.

2a. In the 1980s, however, there was a gentle rise in Belfast's ethnic segregation.

2b. _____

_____

3a. Reports show a <u>marked increase</u> in interest in after-school programs in two-income households during the 1970s and 1980s.

3b. _____

_____

4a. We have seen <u>substantial growth</u> in distance and online education in higher education during the past decade.

4b. _____

_____

Exercise 17

In each item, Sentence A contains an underlined clause (subject + verb). Complete Sentence B by changing the underlined clause into a phrase containing an adjective of degree or speed, a noun form of the verb, and any additional information from the original clause. The first one has been done for you as an example.

1A. Business <u>use</u> of online authoring tools—such as Google Drive, Basecamp, and Trello—<u>has risen more than 200% in just the past decade</u>.

1B. <u>This swift rise in use</u> has allowed people from around the globe to collaborate on projects much more efficiently.

2A. Tomato plant <u>yields dropped by 25%</u> from the previous year despite robust flowering.

2B. Given this _____, the tomato plants may have experienced blossom drop, a condition in which temperature ranges impede fruit production.

3A. Middle-aged women in an experimental group who engaged in a weight-training exercise <u>gained bone density at up to two times the rate</u> of those who engaged in only cardio exercise.

3B. Such a _____ provides support for increased weight-bearing exercise for women over the age of 50.

4A. During the past decade in the U.S., food <u>prices have increased little by little</u> every year.

4B. Despite this _____, the total percentage of salary Americans use for food purchases remains one of the lowest in all developed countries.

5A. Over the last two days, <u>tensions have escalated</u> as the two countries ended negotiations, recalled their diplomats, and even started amassing troops on their shared border.

5B. The _____ have alarmed governments across the region.

Exercise 18

Each sentence contains one error based on word forms. Underline each incorrect word form. Then write the correct form in the blank. The first one has been done for you as an example.

1. The goal of sustainable architecture is to <u>substantial</u> minimize the negative environmental impact of buildings.

   _____
   substantially

2. The most well-known strategy is the installation of solar panels, the price of which has drop sharply in recent years.

   _____

3. But even simple changes in building design can noticeable improve energy savings. _____

4. For example, windows can be positioned to dramatically maximum the input of heat-creating light while substantially minimizing the loss of heat through glass.

   _____

5. Such methods can lead to significant gains in efficiency and dramatic reduces in energy costs. _____

Using Change-of-State Modifiers with Nouns

Another way in which writers express change-of-state involves using *–ing* and *–ed* words to describe the item that is changing. This technique allows writers to pack more information into sentences and to give the reader more information about the impact or context of the change.

Look at these sentences about the economy:

Let's look at another example:

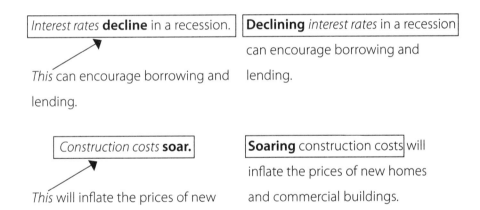

Exercise 19

Transform each sentence in Part A into an *–ing* + noun phrase and place it into the sentence in Part B to create a new sentence in Part C. Note that Sentence 4 requires two such phrases to create the new sentence. The first one has been done for you as an example.

1A. Water resources are dwindling.

1B. Farmers and city governments are fighting over *this* during the drought.

1C. Farmers and city governments are fighting over dwindling water resources during the drought.

2A. Violence is escalating in PG-13 films.

2B. *This* has come to the attention of many parent groups, which are beginning to question the rating system.

2C. _____

_____

3A. Over the past 20 years, college tuition has skyrocketed.

3B. Current students report that *this* has placed a college education out of reach for students.

3C. _____

_____

4A. Readership is declining and budgets are shrinking.

4B. As more and more people get their news from the internet, many newspapers face serious consequences, including *these*.

4C. _____

_____

Chapter 3: Writing about Other Types of Change

Chapter 2 examined words that express various kinds of increases and decreases. Chapter 3 focuses on words that express other kinds of changes, many related to the ideas of "getting better" or "getting worse." While some of these words may include the meaning of an increase or a decrease, they differ from the words in Chapter 2 in that they typically have positive or negative connotations. For example, whereas the word *expand* (from Chapter 2), meaning "to get larger," is neutral in its connotation (neither positive nor negative in and of itself), the word *exacerbate* (in this chapter) refers to an already bad situation or feeling growing worse.

> The auto plant's closing exacerbated our town's unemployment problem.
> (The unemployment problem was already bad; the plant closing made it worse.)
>
> Frustration over the lack of immigration reform was exacerbated by the political parties' refusal to cooperate with each other.
> (Frustration is a negative emotion to begin with; it has been made worse by the lack of cooperation.)

Some words introduced in this chapter express changes that are not concerned with things getting either better or worse but rather with other sorts of transformations. As examples, the word *modify* describes a partial change in something, while the word *convert* describes a change to a different form or property.

Raising Language Awareness

Exercise 1

Words expressing increases and decreases from Chapter 2 are underlined. Circle words that express other kinds of changes. The number of words to be circled is given in parentheses. The first passage has been done for you as an example.

1. In measuring inflation, economists omit consumer items whose costs (fluctuate) greatly, either <u>rising</u> or <u>declining</u> sharply, from month to month. Items that (vary) widely in price include airline tickets and televisions. (2)

2. The altering of photographs, known as photo manipulation, has been practiced since the early 20th century. However, through digital technology, the practice has <u>mushroomed</u> in recent years. Commonly referred to by its slang term *photo-shopping*, photo manipulation is often used to enhance an individual's physical appearance through alterations such as adjusting eye color. (6)

3. After Hurricane Katrina, ecological engineers attempted to create landscapes that would help to restore water quality. In these and other ways, they hope to mitigate the effects of present and past storms. (2)

4. Critics of some current drug use laws contend that the laws have done little to lessen the drug problems. Instead, they argue that these laws have <u>inflated</u> the prison population with individuals who pose no serious threat to society. This population only aggravates existing problems with overcrowding, worsening conditions for all. Indeed, the <u>surging</u> prison population in many states has become a serious social and economic issue. (2)

5. Sound, or audio, files on computers tend to be very large. Thus, they are often <u>compressed</u> for storage. This conversion may result in <u>reduced</u> file quality as the complexity of the data will be simplified. (2)

6. There is <u>mounting</u> evidence that children's creative play has <u>declined</u> as a result of <u>extended</u> periods of watching television and video games. Some researchers believe this <u>decline</u> in play may transform children's cognitive development and modify their skills in social interactions. (2)

Exercise 2

Each set of words contains four verbs that express types of change. Circle the word whose meaning is significantly different from the other three. The first one has been done for you as an example.

1. a. adapt	b. adjust	c. fluctuate	d. modify
2. a. complicate	b. enhance	c. enrich	d. refine
3. a. degenerate	b. deteriorate	c. simplify	d. worsen
4. a. alter	b. convert	c. revitalize	d. transform

3.1 VERBS EXPRESSING CHANGE IN FORM OR BEHAVIOR

A variety of verbs in academic writing express the ways in which people, places, or things change. This section discusses verbs that are neutral in connotation though they may take on positive or negative meanings when used in combination with other words and phrases. One example is the verb *revise*. It is often used with a positive meaning, but in and of itself, it is not necessarily a synonym for *improve*. One could, for instance, revise an opinion of someone in a negative direction.

Raising Language Awareness

Exercise 3

Common verbs that can express changes in form or behavior are listed in Table 3.1. Put a **+** in the blank next to all of the verbs in the list whose meanings you are familiar with and that you use in your own writing. Put a **√** next to those words whose meanings you are familiar with but that you only rarely use. Put a **−** in the blank next to words you are less familiar with.

Table 3.1: Common Verbs That Express Change in Form or Behavior

___ adapt	___ convert	___ revise
___ adjust	___ fluctuate	___ transform
___ alter	___ manipulate	___ vary
___ amend	___ modify	

Building Your Knowledge

In reference to people, change-of-state verbs can involve changes in behavior, beliefs, or attitudes, as shown in the examples:

> With the help of an academic counselor, he <u>modified</u> his study habits.

> New immigrants must <u>adjust</u> to many changes in their lifestyles.

> Employers look for workers with the ability to <u>adapt</u> to different situations.

> The study caused them to <u>transform</u> their thinking about global warming.

As for places and things, change-of-state verbs can indicate additions, deletions, substitutions, or complete changes from one thing to another, as reflected in these examples:

> After receiving further feedback, they <u>altered</u> several points in their proposal.

> Congress voted yesterday to <u>amend</u> the bill.

> They <u>manipulated</u> the visual displays to make them easier to see.

> We then <u>converted</u> the raw scores from our analysis into standard scores.

Change-of-state verbs may occur as main verbs or infinitives (*to* + verb). All of the verbs in Table 3.1 can be transitive—followed by objects (*study habits*, *many changes*, the *visual displays*, etc.). Some are also used intransitively and are followed by prepositional phrases (*adapt to, adjust to*).

Nouns that often follow some of the common change-of-state verbs are listed in Table 3.2.

Table 3.2: Change-of-State Verbs with Object Collocations

Verb	Direct Object Collocation
adapt	behavior, conditions, learning, material, techniques, systems, strategies, international patent law, consultation styles, work routines
adjust	an argument, an approach, expectations, ideas, actions, a program, policies, strategies, tactics, rates, sample size
alter	plans, beliefs, understanding, approaches, a position, a course, a system, dress, relations, disease process, risks, tendencies, the findings of a study
amend	documents, a rule, a law, a statute, a building code, a bill, the constitution, the law of supply and demand, terms, the privacy policy, a statement
modify	approaches, agendas, systems, environments, landscapes, ecosystems resources, instruction, a research question, hardware and software, types of crops, risky behavior, impressions
revise	documents, a hypothesis, a model, texts, strategies, assumptions, concepts, guidelines, policies, rules, standards, projects

Data from COCA.

Table 3.3: Change-of-State Verbs with Prepositional Phrase Collocations

Intransitive Verb	Object of Preposition Collocation
adapt to +	surroundings, circumstances, organizational changes, sweeping changes, ideas, changing consumer tastes, environmental changes, rising temperatures, global warming
adjust to +	life, varying pressures, new challenges, unexpected outcomes, changing conditions, stressful events, surroundings, fluctuations in sales
adjust for +	factors, differences, probabilities, variables

Data from COCA.

Two of the verbs, *adapt* and *adjust,* are frequently used as intransitive verbs and are often followed by *to* + a noun phrase. The verb *adjust* is also followed by *for* + a noun phrase. Collocations for these two verbs are listed in Table 3.3.

Exercise 4

Use Tables 3.2 and 3.3 to answer the questions.

1. Which 3 verbs in Table 3.2 can describe changes in approaches?

_____

2. Which 2 verbs in Table 3.2 can describe change in behavior?

_____

3. Which verb in Table 3.2 can refer to change in the progress of a disease?

_____

4. Which verb in Table 3.3 is used most often to describe changes needed in response to environmental factors?

_____

5. Which verb in Table 3.3 seems most useful for describing statistical changes that are prompted by various conditions?

_____

Exercise 5

Write three *wh*-questions, each containing a change-of-state verb, to which a classmate could respond. Try to use change-of-state verbs in your answers where appropriate. Exchange your questions with those of a classmate and write responses to each other's questions. Example: Q: How are you adjusting to your new job? A: It has been hard to adjust. I have had to modify my work habits.

Convert/Transform + Noun Phrase + *into* + Noun Phrase

Two verbs in this section, *convert* and *transform*, often occur in a grammar pattern that other verbs typically do not. These verbs can describe a complete or significant change of something from one form into another. While they both describe changes in form, quality, or appearance, the verb *convert* tends to express a change from one thing to another for a particular purpose or use, while *transform* may be an unintended change.

To express these ideas, the phrase often has this structure:

[verb] + [noun phrase] + *into* + [noun phrase]

Two examples are:

The facility converts [silicon wafers] into [microprocessors].

In some areas, aggressive trees and shrubs have transformed [bogs] into [forested habitats].

Exercise 6

Use vocabulary context clues to match the phrases in Column A with those in Column B that contain *convert* and *transform* to make complete sentences. The first one has been done for you as an example.

A	B
_d_ 1. With the aging population, we may see some college campuses	a. transform the information they receive into skills that they use.
___ 2. Forage fish and other small fish	b. could easily convert into cash.
___ 3. Teachers must help students	c. need to convert them into a different format.
___ 4. During a supernova explosion, pairs of mirror electrons and mirror positrons	d. converted into retirement communities.
___ 5. In order to upload files, students	e. can convert into acidic runoff that is deadly to plants and animals.
___ 6. Along with scientists, China's political leaders	f. are often converted into fishmeal used to grow salmon, shrimp, or other species.
___ 7. The employees were compensated with securities, which they	g. hope to transform the country into a leading center of innovation.
___ 8. When coal mines close, they often leave behind water and minerals that bacteria	h. would convert into ordinary electrons and positrons.

Vary + Noun Phrase + Preposition + Noun Phrase

The verb *vary* is followed by a remarkable number of prepositions in academic English, depending on meaning and context. It is unusual for a verb to collocate with so many different prepositions. For example, the preposition that most often follows the verb *fluctuate* is *between*, as in *his mood fluctuated between good and bad*. However, prepositions that can follow *vary* include *across, among, between, by, in, on, from,* and *with* or *within*. Some examples adapted from the Corpus of Contemporary American English follow.

Population densities <u>vary across</u> the country.

The sources of black carbon <u>vary by</u> region.

Study abroad programs may <u>vary in</u> length from a full semester to a year.

Estimates <u>vary on</u> the number of viewers for the Super Bowl.

The typical concerns and interests of young adults <u>vary with</u> their age, the influence of their parents, and socioeconomic status.

With *vary* + *by*, we often see [noun phrase] + *by* + [noun phrase] structures. For example, something might vary *state by state*, *region by region*, or *school by school*, etc.

Similarly, with *vary* + *from*, we use many **chunked expressions** in the *from* [noun phrase] *to* [noun phrase] structure. Some examples include *from person to person, from year to year,* and *from study to study*.

Exercise 7

For each sentence with *vary* + preposition, circle the choice that would **not** be correct in meaning or grammatical form. Discuss your choices. The first one has been done for you as an example.

1. Temperatures in this region vary with (a) altitude (b) large animals (c) proximity to large bodies of water (d) density of vegetation.

2. Native American tribes vary in

   (a) language (b) customs

   (c) land (d) culture.

3. Researchers found that gender roles for their subjects varied across

   (a) cultures (b) religious backgrounds

   (c) educational levels (d) learning strategies.

4. The students' opinions on goals of education varied by

   (a) clothing style (b) class level (c) gender (d) field of study.

5. Americans' opinions vary on

   (a) the risks of using fracking to release oil reserves

   (b) the cost of tuition is rising in colleges

   (c) the protection of great white sharks as an endangered species

   (d) the development of massive open online courses (MOOCs) in higher education.

3.2 VERBS EXPRESSING POSITIVE AND NEGATIVE CHANGES

As discussed previously, many of the verbs in this chapter express changes with either positive or negative connotations. *Exacerbate* is an example of making a bad situation or feeling worse. An example of a verb with positive connotations is *reform*, which usually means to improve, correct, or perhaps update something, such as a policy or law.

Raising Language Awareness

Exercise 8

Verbs that can express positive or negative changes are listed in Table 3.4. Put a **+** in the blank next to all of the verbs in the list whose meanings you are familiar with and that you use in your own writing. Put a √ next to those words whose meanings you are familiar with but that you may only rarely use. Put a − in the blank next to words you are less familiar with.

Table 3.4: Verbs That Express Positive or Negative Changes

___ aggravate	___ degenerate	___ exacerbate	___ restore
___ alleviate	___ deteriorate	___ mitigate	___ revitalize
___ complicate	___ enhance	___ refine	___ simplify
___ decline*	___ enrich	___ renew	___ worsen

---

* In Chapter 2, *decline* was presented with its meaning "a downward movement." Here it is considered with its meaning "negative change."

Building Your Knowledge

Using Verbs That Express Changes for Positive, Neutral, or Negative Conditions, Processes, or Activities

A number of verbs express positive or negative changes for things that may be either positive, negative, or neutral. Some examples are presented.

> The clear instructions <u>simplified</u> the process of assembling the cabinet.
> (a positive effect on a neutral process, making the process easier)

> Her grandfather's excellent health suddenly <u>declined</u>.
> (a negative change in a positive condition)

> The new housing complex <u>revitalized</u> the impoverished neighborhood.
> (a positive change in a negative condition)

Note from these examples that, like other verbs you have encountered in this chapter, some verbs are transitive with an object (X *simplified* Y) but others are intransitive without an object (X *declined*).

Some object collocations from COCA that follow some of the transitive change-related verbs are shown in Table 3.5.

For verbs that are sometimes or always intransitive (that are not followed by an object), some frequent subjects that may occur before them are listed in Table 3.6.

Table 3.5: Object Collocations with Transitive Verbs

Verb	Object Collocations
complicate	a situation, matters, tasks
enhance	abilities, reasoning powers, an outlook, understanding, status, longevity
enrich	society, programs, academic quality, lives of everyone, student learning, perspectives
refine	goals, a vision, skills, outcomes, definitions, concepts, the knowledge base, protocols
renew	acts, beliefs, sense of purpose, a sense of self worth, a commitment, public support, hope, energy
restore	peace, faith, confidence, dignity, balance, prosperity, order, native habitats, ecosystems
revitalize	a flagging economy, a country's purpose and standing, public spaces, languages, the integrity of cultures, the peace process
simplify	a process, a task, instructions, a description, a presentation, the problem, the issue, the interpretation

Data from COCA.

Table 3.6: Subject Collocations with Intransitive Verbs

Subject Collocations	Verb
civilizations, educational resources, health, muscle mass, environments, motivation, achievement	**decline**
understanding, arguments, the body, cells, neurons, energy states	**degenerate**
health, mental functions, relationships, economic conditions, assets, buildings, roads, water quality	**deteriorate**

Data from COCA.

Exercise 9

Sort the verbs from Tables 3.5 and 3.6 into the chart to distinguish those that generally express making or becoming better and those that express making or becoming worse. Two have been done for you as examples.

complicate	enhance	restore
decline	enrich	revitalize
degenerate	refine	simplify
deteriorate	renew	

Verbs That Express Making or Becoming Better	Verbs That Express Making or Becoming Worse
enhance	complicate

Exercise 10

Answer the questions.

1. What three prefixes are used in Exercise 9? What does each prefix mean? Use a dictionary if necessary.

   Prefix   Meaning

   a. _____   _____

   b. _____   _____

   c. _____   _____

2. Considering the noun phrases in Table 3.5 following *enhance* and *enrich*, which one refers more to improving individual qualities? Which one refers more to groups of people?

   _____   _____

3. Which verb in Table 3.5 describing positive change tends to refer most specifically to environmental conditions?

   _____

4. Of the verbs expressing negative changes in Table 3.6, which one seems to allow the most diversity in the conditions or situations it can describe?

   _____

Exercise 11

Discuss these questions with a partner or a small group. Use the underlined verbs in your responses.

1. Consider an athletic, musical, or academic skill you have. What are some things you could do to <u>refine</u> this skill?

2. What courses would you like to see added to the curriculum to <u>enhance</u> it? Why do you think these courses would <u>enhance</u> your curriculum?

3. What evidence do you see of environmental conditions that are <u>deteriorating</u> in your community?

4. What are some things you think could <u>complicate</u> the relationship between a college student and his or her parents?

Using Verbs That Express Intensifying or Lessening of Negative Conditions or Situations

The verbs highlighted in the previous section can be used to describe changes in situations or conditions that are positive, negative, or neutral. The verbs in this section typically express changes affecting only negative conditions or situations. Table 3.7 (page 68) shows examples of these verbs with object collocations.

Table 3.7: Object Collocations with Verbs Related to Change in Negative Conditions

Verb	Object Collocations
aggravate	traffic congestion, an existing negative condition, existing negative relations, existing problems, pain, misery, inflammatory responses, disease symptoms
alleviate	anxiety, concerns, fears, hunger, pain, crises, damage, financial strain, economic troubles, tensions
exacerbate	conflict, difficulties, the problem, the gap between rich and poor, a large market decline, existing health problems, existing tensions, your work stress, the loss of biodiversity
mitigate	bias, effects of climate change, inequalities, problems, negative consequences of global trade, the fallout from the recession, threats
worsen	drought conditions, poor health, strained relations, a tense political atmosphere, a crisis, the economy, poverty

Data from COCA.

Exercise 12

Use a dictionary and information from Table 3.7 to answer these questions.

1. Which two verbs express the meaning of lessening a negative condition or state?

   _____   _____

2. Which verb making a negative condition or state better tends to occur more often with emotional conditions?

   _____

3. Which three verbs express the meaning of intensifying a negative condition or state?

   _____   _____

   _____

4. Of the verbs that intensify a negative condition or state, which one can also be used when the subject describes what becomes more negative?

   _____

5. In addition to emotions, can you identify a few other general categories for the negative conditions and situations listed in the chart?

   _____

   _____

Exercise 13

Rewrite these sentences adapted from COCA using one of the verbs from Table 3.7 and deleting or changing words as appropriate. Note that the verb may be part of an infinitive (*to* + verb) structure. The first one has been done for you as an example.

1. Privacy concerns can make the already uneasy relationship that many people have with social networks even worse.

   Privacy concerns can exacerbate the already uneasy relationship

   that many people have with social networks.

2. "Children of the Border," a development project that serves people in Haiti and other countries, aims to make problems of unemployment and poverty less severe.

   _____

   _____

   _____

3. Climate change may make existing problems such as degradation of air quality worse than they already are.

_____

_____

4. Some of the streams in the Bristol Bay area are going to be permanently lost, and scientists must find ways to make the consequences of these losses less damaging to the environment.

_____

_____

_____

5. Several World Bank studies indicated that resorting to biofuels could make the extent of world hunger greater than it already is.

_____

_____

_____

3.3 ABSTRACT NOUNS DERIVED FROM VERBS EXPRESSING CHANGE

Building Your Knowledge

Almost all of the verbs discussed in Chapter 3 have abstract noun counterparts that are common in academic writing. Often these abstract nouns are used at the beginning of sentences where they help to create links to previous ideas. In many cases, a verb used in one sentence may be followed by the noun form of that verb.

The doctor <u>adjusted</u> the patient's medication to a lower dosage for two weeks. The <u>adjustment</u> alleviated several negative side effects that had been a problem with the initial dosage.

The abstract noun form may also be used as part of a compound noun form.

> The city council has approved a plan to <u>restore</u> three historical buildings in the center of downtown. This <u>restoration</u> project is expected to increase tourist traffic to the area.

In some cases the abstract noun form may be the same as the verb form (e.g., *decline*). However, most abstract nouns feature the common noun suffixes of *–ment*, *–sion*, or *–tion*.

Exercise 14

Write the abstract noun form for each verb.

Verb	Noun	Verb	Noun	Verb	Noun
adapt		decline		refine	
adjust		degenerate		renew	
aggravate		deteriorate		restore	
alleviate		enhance		revise	
alter		enrich		shift	
amend		manipulate		simplify	
complicate		mitigate		transform	
convert		modify		vary	

In academic English, abstract nouns derived from change-of-state verbs usually have prepositional phrases that modify them and often refer to previous information. Most often the prepositional phrase begins with *of*, describing what changes, as in these examples:

enhancement of existing strategies

renewal of peace negotiations

deterioration of political rights

degeneration of the nervous system

A few of the abstract nouns derived from change-of-state verbs are followed by prepositional phrases that start with prepositions other than *of*, as in these examples:

adaptation to / a new culture

adjustment to a new work schedule

adjustment in the dosage of medicine

conversion to another format

As shown, the abstract noun + prepositional phrases beginning with *to* describe a change to someone or something not mentioned in the phrase (e.g., *someone adapted to a new culture*). The abstract noun + preposition *in* often refers to a change related to the object of the preposition (e.g., *the dosage of medicine*).

However, prepositions other than *of* are not especially common after any of the change abstract nouns. The reason for this is that other prepositions typically describe space (movement or position) or time meanings, while *of* is used to add details as in the earlier examples (e.g., what kind of *enhancement, renewal*, etc.).

Exercise 15

Choose five nouns from the list you created in Exercise 14 that you would like to use more in your writing. Look up each in a concordancer and then, on a separate sheet of paper, list examples of prepositional phrase modifiers that commonly follow each one. An example for *adaptation* has been done for you.

Noun: <u>adaptation</u>
Common prepositions: *of, to, in*
Examples:

of imported ideas and practices
of immigrant youth
of theories of behavior change
to climate change
to different environments
to university life
in a species
in a changing world
in the domain of language

Chapter 4: Writing about Causal Relationships: Connectors and Abstract Nouns

Chapters 4 and 5 focus on the language for expressing cause and effect. Academic writing tasks often involve analyzing processes, problems, solutions, policies, and arguments and presenting your own opinions or results of your own research. Such assignments require that you give the reasoning behind the claims you make and examine the **causes** and **effects** that explain that reasoning. Research shows that academic writers tend to use causal phrases and verbs most often to show these relationships.

Raising Language Awareness

You may be familiar with this set of connectors that introduce reasons or results:

> Fossil fuels are harmful to our environment <u>because</u> they increase global warming and they are not renewable.

> Fossil fuels are harmful to our environment, <u>so</u> scientists are working to find and develop alternative energy sources.

> Eventually, supplies of fossil fuels will be depleted. <u>Therefore</u>, scientists are working to find and develop alternative energy sources.

In academic writing, it is common to use connectors that require a different grammatical environment. These connectors are followed by abstract nouns, which are not necessarily common in everyday spoken English. In order to produce these structures, writers often use noun derivatives of adjectives and verbs.

Exercise 1

For each pair of sentences, bracket the connector that creates a relationship and underline the structure that follows the connector. Discuss the difference between the structures used after each connector in each set. The first pair has been done for you as examples.

1. A. Scientists are working to find and develop alternative energy sources [because] <u>supplies of fossil fuels will eventually be depleted</u>.

   B. Scientists are working to find and develop alternative energy sources [due to] <u>the eventual depletion of fossil fuels.</u>

2. A. Even though there are many reasons to support the use of nuclear energy, many people reject nuclear energy as unsafe.

   B. Despite the many reasons to support the use of nuclear energy, many people reject nuclear energy as unsafe.

3. A. Although nuclear power might be dangerous, some scientists and environmentalists still favor this resource.

   B. Even with the dangers of nuclear power, some scientists and environmentalists still favor this resource.

4. A. The creation of nuclear power contributes very little to global warming because the emissions of greenhouse gases are low.

   B. The creation of nuclear power contributes very little to global warming given the low emissions of greenhouse gases.

4.1 USING CONNECTORS AND ABSTRACT NOUNS

Building Your Knowledge

Certain causal connectors (*so, because, therefore*) are often used repeatedly in speech. Academic writers often use noun phrases to make their sentences more concise and to place focus on key information. This section shows how writers can achieve those goals by transforming entire sentences or clauses into abstract noun phrases.

All the connectors in Sentence A in Exercise 1 are followed by subjects and verbs called **dependent clauses**. However, all the connectors in Sentence B in are followed by **abstract noun phrases**: derivatives of verbs (*deplete* → *depletion*) or adjectives (*dangerous* → *danger*) and other additional information.

Forming Abstract Noun Phrases

Abstract noun phrases allow writers to transform entire sentences into phrases that they can use inside a larger sentence.

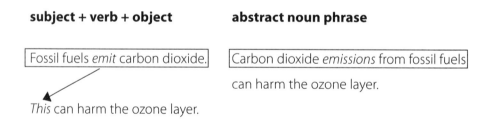

subject + verb + object

Fossil fuels *emit* carbon dioxide.

This can harm the ozone layer.

abstract noun phrase

Carbon dioxide *emissions* from fossil fuels can harm the ozone layer.

Table 4.1 lists causal connectors that are followed by abstract noun phrases. Writers use these structures to show complex relationships between ideas.

Table 4.1: Causal Connectors That Introduce Abstract Noun Phrases

Meaning-Relationship	Connectors	Examples with Common Collocations
Showing the result or effect of previous ideas	**as a result of**	Low-income families are struggling to put food on the table **as a result of** sharp <u>increases</u> in food prices.
	because of	**Because of** recent <u>concerns</u> about food safety, the Food and Drug Administration is considering new guidelines for meat-packing plants.
	due to	The company was able to hire additional employees **due to** phenomenal <u>sales</u> during the first quarter.
	given	**Given** <u>the need</u> for professional nurses, Jenna decided to attend a nursing program after college.
	in light of	New jobs are opening in many corporations **in light of** current <u>interest</u> in green technology.
	thanks to (often positive)	**Thanks to** <u>declines</u> in unemployment, consumer confidence has increased.
	on account of (note: often reserved for very formal situations)	Several farms were forced to destroy their crops **on account of** *E. coli* <u>infestation</u>.
Introducing a result not influenced by a previous factor	**despite** (note: Not *despite of*)	**Despite** sales <u>gains</u> in the domestic market, our losses in foreign markets have created a deficit.
	in spite of	The U.S. ranks 26th in the world in health systems **in spite of** the country's <u>wealth</u>.
	even with (note: a comma is used even when the connector is in the middle of the sentence)	**Even with** the <u>election</u> of the country's first black president, many people believe that racism is still a major issue in the U.S.
		Many people believe that racism is still a major issue in the U.S., **even with** the <u>election</u> of the country's first black president.

Using Connectors with Abstract Noun Phrases

Writers use several strategies involving connectors and abstract noun phrases to show causal relationships. Using connectors with abstract nouns allows writers to reduce the number of *to be* forms by changing adjectives into nouns.

connector + subject + *to be* + adjective	**connector + abstract noun from adjective**
Class was canceled yesterday [because] the instructor was *ill.*	Class was canceled yesterday [due to] instructor *illness.*

Another way to reduce *to be* forms is to cut *there is / there are*.

connector + *there is / are* + noun	**connector + noun phrase**
[Even though] there are *many reasons* to support the use of nuclear energy, many people reject nuclear energy as unsafe.	[Despite] *many reasons* to support the use of nuclear energy, many people reject nuclear energy as unsafe.

Using connectors with abstract noun phrases can also reduce the number of weaker verbs such as *to have* needed to form a clause. They can also help writers reduce wordiness and repetition, as shown:

connector + subject + *have*	**connector + noun phrase**
The recent college graduate was offered a relatively high-paying job [because] he had a lot of *educational research experience*.	The recent college graduate was offered a relatively high-paying job [on account of] his considerable *educational and research experience*.

In the sentence in the left column, *he* acts as the subject for the verb *had*. In the sentence in the right column, *his* acts as a modifier for the noun *experience*. Similarly, in the second example, the proper noun *John* in the left column acts as the subject for the verb *had*, while the possessive form *John's* in the right column acts as a modifier for the noun *experience*.

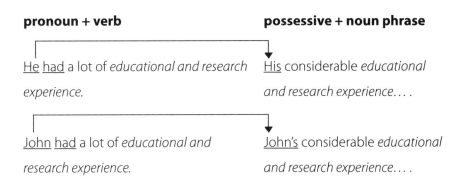

pronoun + verb   **possessive + noun phrase**

He had a lot of *educational and research*   His considerable *educational*
experience.   *and research experience.* . . .

John had a lot of *educational and*   John's considerable *educational*
research experience.   *and research experience.* . . .

Using phrases instead of clauses can, in some cases, allow writers to reduce the use of passive voice:

connector + subject + passive verb   **connector + noun phrase**

[Because] *new survey data* were   [In light of] *new survey data,*
generated, media sources can no longer   media sources can no longer
project which candidate will win the   project which candidate will
election.   win the election.

Exercise 2

Causal connectors followed by clauses (subjects + verbs) appear in these sentences. Transform the information in the underlined clause into an abstract noun phrase using the connector provided. Be sure to make any other necessary revisions based on the examples on pages 78 and 79. The first one has been done for you as an example.

1. a. Because <u>new evidence was found</u>, the prosecution has dropped all charges against the arrested man.

   b. In light of <u>new evidence</u>, the prosecution has dropped all charges against the arrested man.

2. a. Many doctors now advise their patients on what foods they should eat because <u>there is a relationship between diet and heart disease</u>.

   b. Many doctors now advise their patients on what foods they should eat given _____

   _____.

3. a. Although <u>he was dissatisfied with the results</u>, he felt he learned a great deal from doing the experiment.

   b. Despite _____

   _____, he felt he learned a great deal from doing the experiment.

4. a. Given that <u>the organization has a strong track record of success</u>, its proposal for additional funding was approved.

   b. As a result of _____

   _____, its proposal for additional funding was approved.

5. a. The new version of our smart phone outsold competitors' versions because <u>it has a sharper and clearer screen</u>.

   b. The new version of our smart phone outsold competitors' versions thanks to _____

   _____.

6. a. Even though <u>the client was interested in our concept</u>, we lost the bid to another company, whose idea was considered more cutting-edge.

  b. In spite of_____

  _____, we lost the bid to another company, whose idea was considered more cutting-edge.

4.2 MODIFYING ABSTRACT NOUN PHRASES

Building Your Knowledge

When writers change verb forms into noun forms, they need to be sure all modifiers agree.

connector + subject + verb	connector + noun phrase
Scientists are working to find and develop alternative energy sources [because] fossil fuels *will* <u>eventually</u> *be depleted.*	Scientists are working to find and develop alternative energy sources [because of] the <u>eventual</u> *depletion* of fossil fuels.

The adverb (*eventually*) in the first sentence becomes an adjective (*eventual*) in the second sentence because *eventual* is modifying a noun (*depletion*), not a verb (*deplete*). Thus, an adjective form is needed.

adverb + verb	adjective + abstract noun

Fossil fuels will *eventually* be depleted.   . . . the *eventual* depletion of fossil fuels.

A writer must also pay attention to word order. Adverbs can come before or after the main verb.

connector + subject + verb

> Because jobs that require a college degree have <u>increased dramatically</u>, college enrollments have risen.

> Because jobs that require a college degree have <u>dramatically increased</u>, college enrollments have risen.

Adjectives come before the nouns.

> Because of the <u>dramatic increase</u> in jobs that require a college degree, college enrollments have risen.

Exercise 3

Causal connectors followed by clauses (subjects + verbs) appear in these sentences. Transform the information in the underlined clause into an abstract noun phrase by changing the verb or adjective into a noun. Be sure to make any other necessary revisions, such as changing word order or word forms. Use the connector, the underlined forms, and forms of the italicized words to build the new phrase. The first one has been done for you as an example.

1. A. Since <u>cell phone applications have been *developing rapidly*</u>, many people can now run their businesses entirely by phone.

   B. In light of <u>rapid developments in cell phone applications,</u> many people can now run their businesses entirely by phone.

2. A. The town has received a recommendation from the state government because <u>it *fought successfully* to keep its streets free of crime.</u>

   B. The town has received a recommendation from the state government as a result of _____

   _____ .

3. A. I would like to study contract law in your program because <u>I am *very interested* in how the internet has increased access to music online.</u>

   B. I would like to study contract law in your program given

   _____

   _____ .

4. A. Because <u>you *responded* to our request *promptly*</u>, we have been able to solve the client's software issue before further damage occurred.

   B. Thanks to _____

   _____, we have been able to solve the client's software issue before further damage occurred.

5. A. Even though <u>the client became *extremely angry*</u>, the customer care staff maintained a professional attitude and attended to the client's needs.

   B. Despite _____

   _____, the customer care staff maintained a professional attitude and attended to the client's needs.

Describing Abstract Nouns

Look at Number 3 in Exercise 3. In Sentence A, the word *very* described the adjective *interested*. *Very* is an adverb, so it cannot describe a noun, like *interest*.

The most common way to express the ideas "very" or "a lot" when describing a noun is the word *great*.

very + adjective	*great* + abstract noun
I am *very interested* in how the internet has increased access to music online.	My *great interest* is how the internet has increased access to music online.

Exercise 4

List some other words that are used as synonyms and antonyms for the word *great*. Remember to check which words collocate with the word *interest*. Look up the word *interest* in a learner dictionary, collocations dictionary, or online concordancer for ideas. The first one in each list has been done for you as an example.

Synonyms:

1. great interest   3.   5.

2.   4.   6.

Antonyms:

1. little interest   3.

2.   4.

Adding Prepositions

Sometimes when creating abstract noun phrases, writers must add prepositions. Some verbs do not take prepositions, but their related abstract nouns do.

verb + object   **abstract noun + preposition + object**

We *solved* the problem.   Our *solution to* the problem . . .

Verbs and nouns that follow this pattern are listed in Table 4.2. If more than one preposition is listed, the first is more frequently used in academic writing. Each abstract noun takes a preposition, but its related verb does not.

Table 4.2: Transitive Verbs Whose Abstract Noun Derivatives Require Prepositions

Verb + No Preposition	Noun + Preposition	Verb + No Preposition	Noun + Preposition
affect	an effect on	impact	an impact on
answer	an answer to	improve	an improvement in
approach	an approach to	increase	an increase in
attack	an attack on	influence	an influence on
benefit	a benefit to/for	lack	a lack of
contact	contact with	need	a need for
control	control over	oppose	an opposition to
cure	a cure for	prefer	a preference for
decrease	a decrease in	reduce	a reduction in
delay	a delay in	request	a request for
demand	demand for	research	research on/into
desire	desire for	resemble	a resemblance to
discuss	a discussion of/about	respect	respect for
emphasize	emphasis on	solve	a solution to/for
enter	entry into	support	support for

Exercise 5

For each blank in the paragraph, decide if you should add a preposition. If yes, write the correct preposition from the list in the blank. More than one answer may be correct. If no, write an X in the blank. The first two have been done for you as examples.

Prepositions:	for	in	of	on	to	with

Dear Neighbors:

While the general public does not often make direct contact with its elected city officials, I urge you to contact _X_ them today. I have written to our officials numerous times to request _____ road maintenance in our neighborhood, but I have not received any answer _____ my inquiries. We all know that the current economic situation has resulted in a decrease _____ revenues for the city. We understand that that the city lacks _____ money. But our neighborhood has experienced great increases _____ both housing and commercial development over the past five years, which has increased city revenues contributed from our neighborhood. Increased road use has affected _____ the quality of road surfaces: some roads are so full of potholes that they pose a safety risk. We demand _____ improvements _____ road surfaces immediately! Our demand _____ improvements must be heard! Please show your support _____ this demand by writing your officials today.

Exercise 6

Casual connectors followed by clauses (subjects + verbs) appear in these sentences. Transform the information in the underlined clause into an abstract noun phrase by changing the verb or adjective into a noun. Be sure to make any other necessary revisions, including adding prepositions. The first one has been done for you as an example.

1. a. Although <u>the governor supported the initiative</u>, it could not garner enough public support to pass.

   b. In spite of <u>the governor's support for the initiative</u>, it could not garner enough public support to pass.

2. a. Union members voted against the initiative because <u>the government demanded higher insurance premiums</u>.

   b. Union members voted against the initiative as a result of

   _____

   _____ .

3. a. Businesses opposed the initiative because <u>it lacked safeguards against increased corporate taxes</u>.

   b. Businesses opposed the initiative given _____

   _____ .

4. a. And, in general, the public did not favor the bill <u>because it decreased public services like welfare</u>.

   b. And, in general, the public did not favor the bill because of

   _____

   _____ .

4.3 PUNCTUATING CAUSAL PHRASES

Building Your Knowledge

Writers separate a causal phrase at the beginning of a sentence from the rest of the sentence with a comma. The comma is usually not necessary if the causal phrase comes at the end of the sentence. An exception is the phrase *even with*, which introduces a result not influenced by a previous factor. See Table 4.3 for examples.

Table 4.3: Comma Use with Causal Phrases

Beginning Placement with Comma	End Placement with No Comma
Clause	Clause
[*Because*] they increase global warming and they are not renewable, fossil fuels are harmful to our environment.	Fossil fuels are harmful to our environment [*because*] they increase global warming and they are not renewable.
Abstract Noun Phrase	Abstract Noun Phrase
[*In light of*] rapid developments in cell phone applications, many people can now run their businesses entirely by phone.	Many people can now run their businesses entirely by phone [*in light of*] rapid developments in cell phone applications.

Exercise 7

Check the punctuation in each sentence. Add commas where necessary.

1. Given that two-income families earn the same income today as single-income families did in the 1950s the option for stay-at-home mothers or fathers is diminishing.

2. The results of the study were viewed with some skepticism given the small sample size.

3. As a result of our collaboration with a university writing instructor we propose substantial changes to the current college preparatory classes offered in our program.

4. Families are now facing higher prices for meat and milk because of increased prices for corn and fuel.

5. It has been a very good year for sales of our local newspaper even with the increase in cover price.

Chapter 5: Writing about Causal Relationships: Verbs

Chapter 4 introduced connectors and related vocabulary that can help writers create concise, sophisticated sentences to express causes or effects. Chapter 5 introduces strong, academic verbs that writers can use to achieve similar goals. It also highlights the characteristics of these verbs, especially collocations (the prepositions that link with these verbs and academic vocabulary that precedes or follows these verbs), frequency of use, and grammatical environments, so that you can feel more confident about using this vocabulary in your own writing.

Raising Language Awareness

Exercise 1

Read the passage. Underline all the verbs and any linked prepositions that express a cause-effect relationship. The number of cause-effect verbs in each paragraph is given in parentheses. The first one has been done as an example.

Sleep <u>affects</u> many areas of our lives: work, relationships, decision-making, and general well-being. Recent studies have focused on the topic of sleep, noting that inadequate amounts of sleep can lead to poor health and weight gain and can also inhibit one's productivity. It can even account for increased accidents on the road. (4)

Several factors may contribute to sleep disorders. Some disorders can be attributed to age and our circadian rhythms, which regulate our internal clocks. As we grow older, our internal clocks are no longer synchronized with the day-night cycle and our bodies want us to go to sleep early and rise even earlier. Gender may also account for sleep disorders, as some studies suggest that women are more likely to suffer from insomnia, though results are somewhat inconclusive. (3)

Overall, many studies show that it is lifestyle issues that most influence our sleep patterns. The invention of the light bulb now allows us to remain awake and work late into the night. Our consumption of caffeine enables us to trick our internal clocks and prevent sleep. Finally, overtime promotes more work, which triggers more stress, further hindering our sleep and rendering us irritable and unfocused. (7)

Exercise 2

Circle the verb or verb phrase that has a meaning significantly different from the others in each set of verbs that expresses a causal relationship.

1. a. curb   b. deter   c. provoke   d. suppress

2. a. enable   b. induce   c. inhibit   d. promote

3. a. block   b. create   c. evoke   d. generate

4. a. bring about   b. contribute to   c. lead to   d. stem from

5. a. enable   b. spark   c. stimulate   d. trigger

5.1 USING VERBS THAT INTRODUCE REASONS OR CAUSES

Building Your Knowledge

Many verbs can introduce causes or reasons, but they cannot be used interchangeably. Thus, although looking up words in a thesaurus can help students find alternatives to avoid repetition, this can be a dangerous strategy if used on its own. As outlined in Chapter 1, writers need to **investigate the characteristics of the alternatives** in order to know how to use them accurately in their writing. Some of the most frequent nouns (or types of nouns) that come before the verb introducing reasons or causes are listed in Table 5.1.

Table 5.1: Subject Collocations with Verbs Introducing Reasons/Causes

Nouns	Verb
problems, issues, difficulties, conflicts, complications	(a)rise from
deaths, success, differences, an increase/decline, growth	be attributed to
pleasure, benefits, satisfaction, income, value(s)	derive from
themes, categories, findings, patterns, conclusions, trends	emerge from
conclusion(s), implications, effects, results, (research) question	follow from
bacteria, nitrogen, lesion, tumors, particles, emissions, rays	originate from
problems, changes, effects/outcomes, injuries, loss(es)	result from
problems, troubles, difficulties, loss, doubt, anger	stem from

Data from COCA.

Exercise 3

Use the information in Table 5.1 to answer the questions.

1. Which verb tends to be used with nouns that hold positive meanings?

   _____

2. Which two verbs tend to be used with nouns that hold negative meanings?

   _____   _____

3. Which two verbs seem to be used with either positive or negative nouns?

   _____   _____

4. What generalization can you make about the nouns that collocate with *originate from*?

   _____

5. What generalization can you make about the nouns that collocate with *emerge from*?

   _____

5.2 USING VERBS THAT INTRODUCE RESULTS OR EFFECTS

There are many verbs that can introduce the results or effects of events, processes, problems, and research—topics that often form the focus of academic writing. This section highlights the characteristics of the contexts in which these verbs are used, focusing specifically on the academic vocabulary that precedes or follows these verbs (collocations).

Building Your Knowledge

Exercise 4

Verbs that can introduce results or effects are listed. Put a **+** in the blank next to all of the verbs in Table 5.2 whose meanings you are familiar with and that you use in your own writing. Put a **√** next to those words whose meanings you are familiar with but that you only rarely use. Put a **−** in the blank next to words you are less familiar with.

Table 5.2: Verbs That Introduce Results or Effects

More Frequent		Less Frequent	
___ account for	___ generate	___ bring about	___ play a role in
___ affect	___ influence	___ evoke	___ prompt
___ allow for	___ lead to	___ give rise to	___ provoke
___ cause	___ produce	___ impact	___ render
___ contribute to	___ promote	___ induce	___ spark
___ create	___ result in	___ motivate	___ trigger
___ develop	___ stimulate	___ perpetuate	
___ enable	___ yield		
___ form			

Data from COCA.

Exercise 5

Some of the most frequent nouns (or types of nouns) that come after three common verbs introducing results or effects are listed. For each verb, describe the types of nouns that follow. The first one has been done for you as an example.

Verb	Nouns That Commonly Follow the Verb
1. generate	a. income, jobs, revenue, profits, cash, sales, money b. electricity, power, heat, energy c. support, controversy, excitement, questions, debate
2. give rise to	a. problems, concerns, questions, conflicts, issues, disputes b. symptoms, disease, cells
3. yield	a. results, scores, findings, information, data, insights, evidence b. servings, cups, calories

Data from COCA.

1a. generate + _positive things having to do with money or the economy_

1b. generate + _____

1c. generate + _____

2a. give rise to + _____

2b. give rise to + _____

3a. yield + _____

3b. yield + _____

Exercise 6

Look up these verbs in a learner dictionary or in COCA. List some of the most common nouns that follow each verb. Then, for each verb, describe the types of nouns that follow.

perpetuate	
provoke	
stimulate	
trigger	

1. perpetuate + _____

_____

2. provoke + _____

_____

3. stimulate + _____

_____

4. trigger + _____

_____

Exercise 7

The most common collocations, including some common grammatical environments for each verb, are listed. Write a sample sentence for each on a separate sheet of paper. If you take a sentence from a dictionary or from COCA, please note your source.

account for	a. actions, behavior, practices b. variance, differences c. a number or amount: half of, the majority of, (approximately) 90% of, a total of
allow for	a. analysis, examination b. development, growth, movement, access, expansion, flexibility c. (the) possibility (of/that)
prompt	a. questions, response, questions, investigation b. government, people, officials, president, congress + to do something
render	a. decision, verdict, judgment b. something + negative adjective (useless, obsolete, vulnerable, ineffective, meaningless)

5.3 USING VERBS THAT EXPRESS HOW A RESULT CAN BE MINIMIZED

Building Your Knowledge

When analyzing processes, problems, policies, and research, writers often need to show how a cause might minimize a particular outcome. Table 5.3 lists common academic verbs used to express this idea.

Table 5.3: Verbs That Introduce How a Result Can Be Minimized

block	hinder	interfere with	restrain
curb	impede	limit	slow
deter	inhibit	prevent	suppress
hamper			

While all of these verbs share a similar meaning, they are used with different collocations. Some are used to show how a positive effect is minimized, and some to show how a negative one is. They can also differ in the grammatical environments in which they can occur in a sentence. It is therefore important to investigate each verb's characteristics.

Exercise 8

Explore common collocations for five of the verbs that introduce how a result can be minimized. Put an X next to the one that is **inappropriate and does not collocate with** the verb. Use your dictionary or other resources if necessary.

Verb	Nouns That Commonly Follow the Verb
1. block	___ *access* to the internet ___ the *implications* of the new law ___ any *efforts* to increase taxes ___ blood *flow*
2. deter	___ any possible *aggression* ___ racist *behavior* ___ *hopes* for peace ___ *violence* in the street
3. hinder	___ the company's *ability* to invest ___ the *production* of new equipment ___ academic *success* ___ *terrorism* at home and abroad
4. impede	___ *efforts* to reduce crime ___ economic *growth* ___ *progress* towards our goal ___ increased *pollution*
5. restrain	___ inappropriate *behavior* ___ the *growth of inflation* ___ economic *recovery* ___ out-of-control *spending*

Exercise 9

Discuss answers to the questions about each verb after reading the sets of sentences with common collocations (underlined).

1. What do you notice about the kind of grammatical structure often used before the verb *curb*?

    a. Members of the environmental team proposed <u>several steps to</u> curb greenhouse gas emissions.

    b. Local police have implemented <u>a number of measures to</u> curb violence.

    c. <u>Efforts to</u> curb email spam via filters have worked.

2. What differences do you notice between *prevent* and the collocations in Items a–c and those in d–e? (*Hint*: Look at the nouns that come before and after <u>prevent</u> in Items d–e.)

    a. This action will prevent <u>further problems</u> from occurring.

    b. The World Health Organization announced a new plan to prevent <u>the spread of disease.</u>

    c. Precautions are now in place that are sufficient to prevent <u>a future oil spill.</u>

    d. Lack of job growth will prevent <u>economic recovery.</u>

    e. His injury prevented him from <u>becoming a successful professional soccer player.</u>

3. What do you notice about the grammatical structures that often follow the verbs *slow* and *accelerate*?

    a. Studies show that flaxseed can slow <u>the growth of tumors.</u>

    b. The "platform frame" style of building construction slows <u>the progress of fire.</u>

    c. The organization hopes that increasing economic security will accelerate <u>the pace of reform.</u>

    d. Elements can enter cracks in the concrete and accelerate <u>the rate of deterioration.</u>

4. What three common types of collocations follow *suppress*?

    a. suppress the growth of bacteria | suppress the spread of the virus

    b. suppress the immune system

    c. suppress dissent | suppress rebellion | suppress anti-government speech or ideas

---

When using effect/result verbs, pay attention to the specific prepositions that collocate with many of them.

Exercise 10

Using a learner dictionary or concordancer, fill in the blanks by adding the correct prepositions.

1. Online music theft has played a big role _____ current changes to copyright laws.

2. The mudslides were blamed _____ the destruction of more than a dozen homes.

3. His severe headache interfered _____ his ability to do well on the exam.

4. Advances in green technology will give rise _____ new jobs.

5. The downturn in the housing market has prevented thousands of families _____ obtaining mortgage loans.

6. New rules for obtaining mortgage loans have contributed _____ an overall decline in the number of loans approved.

7. The collaborative effort by neighbors and police resulted _____ reduced crime.

8. A reduction in car theft resulted _____ the collaborative effort by police and neighbors.

When using verbs to express causal relationships, you also need to be careful that you don't "flipflop" an idea by using a reason verb instead of a result verb. For example: *The rains caused the mudslides,* <u>not</u> *the rains resulted from the mudslides.* Also, be careful to use an active verb, not a passive *be* + verb form, when needed.

Exercise 11

Determine whether each sentence with a cause-effect verb is correct (C) or incorrect (I). Correct the incorrect sentences. The first one has been done for you as an example.

_____I_____ 1. The recent Supreme Court decision was generated much controversy throughout the country.
<u>The recent Supreme Court decision generated much</u>
<u>controversy throughout the country.</u>

_____ 2. Lack of technical knowledge can limit a person's job prospects in the current market.

_____

_____

_____ 3. Patricia's success was derived a lot of hard work and a little bit of luck.

_____

_____

_____ 4. My interest in ancient history really sparked the history course I took.

_____

_____

_____ 5. His rather poor performance can partly be attribute his severe headache.

_____

_____

5.4 CRAFTING SENTENCES WITH CAUSAL VERBS AND ABSTRACT NOUN PHRASES

Chapter 4 helped you build your repertoire of abstract nouns and connectors, which are quite commonly used in academic writing. By using this type of vocabulary, writers can pack the information from an entire clause or sentence into another sentence. This section provides additional practice using abstract nouns with the list of verbs in Chapter 5.

Building Your Knowledge

This example from Chapter 4 illustrates how to create variety and a concise, sophisticated style by using abstract noun phrases in your sentences to show cause/effect.

subject + verb	abstract noun phrase
Scientists are working to find and develop alternative energy sources [because] <u>supplies of fossil fuels will eventually be depleted</u>.	Scientists are working to find and develop alternative energy sources [because of] <u>the eventual depletion of fossil fuel supplies</u>.

Abstract noun phrases can also be used as both subjects and objects of causal verbs.

subject + verb	**abstract noun phrase**
Supplies of fossil fuels *will eventually be depleted.* This **has led to** an increase in research on alternative energy sources.	*The eventual depletion* of fossil fuels **has led to** an increase in research on alternative energy sources.

subject + verb	**abstract noun phrase as object**
Serotonin *is produced.* Complex carbohydrates **stimulate** this.	Complex carbohydrates **stimulate** the *production* of serotonin.

Exercise 12

For each pair of sentences, transform the first sentence into an abstract noun phrase and place this phrase inside the second sentence. The first one has been done for you as an example.

1. a. Serotonin cells are distributed widely.

   b. *This* influences various psychological functions in the body.

   The wide distribution of serotonin cells influences

   various psychological functions in the body.

2. a. An individual is able to engage in daily activities.

   b. Poor eyesight can seriously hinder *this*.

   Poor eyesight can seriously hinder _____

   _____

3 a. Soil erodes and carbon is lost.

   b. Hilly, terraced farmland prevents *this.*

   Hilly, terraced farmland prevents _____

_____ .

4 a. They emit less exhaust and noise.

   b. The use of four-stroke engines for snowmobiles will curb *this.*

   The use of four-stroke engines for snowmobiles will curb

_____

_____ .

5 a. A fire consumes limbs, twigs, and leaves.

   b. *This* can create mudslides on hillsides during the rainy season.

_____

_____ can create mudslides on hillsides

during the rainy season.

This example shows a cause-effect verb with both subject and object abstract noun phrases.

Exercise 13

Transform each clause into an abstract noun phrase based on the underlined words by removing the word *because* and connecting the new phrases with the causal verb given. Make other changes as necessary, such as deleting words or changing word order. The first one has been done for you as an example.

1. In 1965, because U.S. immigration laws <u>changed</u>, a larger number of immigrant families were <u>admitted</u>.

   In 1965, <u>changes in U.S. immigration laws</u> resulted in the <u>admission of a larger number of immigrant families.</u>

2. We <u>support</u> this legislation because we <u>believe</u> in freedom of expression.

   Our _____

   follows from our _____.

3. Because penicillin was <u>discovered</u>, health care has greatly <u>improved</u>.

   The _____

   has brought about _____.

4. Many illnesses have become <u>resistant</u> to drug therapy because people <u>overuse</u> antibiotics.

   The _____

   stems from people's _____.

5. Because a person <u>exercises</u> regularly, ghrelin, an appetite-stimulating hormone meant to protect the body from losing weight too quickly, is <u>released</u>.

   Regular_____ can trigger the _____

   _____.

Exercise 14

Rewrite each passage using the verb in parentheses, making any revisions necessary. Be sure to investigate the meaning and grammatical environments of the verbs. The first one has been done for you as an example. You may need to turn adjectives or verbs into abstract nouns as in the examples on pages 103–104. If the verb in the original sentence introduces an effect, and the verb in the parentheses introduces a cause, you may need to reverse the order of information in the new sentence.

1. If we use fertilizer, the leaves will grow faster. (*promote*)

   Fertilizers promote faster leaf growth.

2. The doctors soon realized that the patient's vision problems caused his chronic headaches. (*be attributed to*)

3. Many in the workforce feel quite anxious when layoffs increase. (*generate*)

4. If we bar the release of coyotes back into the wild, many believe the coyote will become extinct. (*lead to*)

5. Strains of drug-resistant bacteria are causing antibiotics to be ineffective. (*render*)

_____

_____

6. Racial profiling by police caused the community to protest. (*spark*)

_____

_____

Chapter 6: Creating Balance and Emphasis with Parallel Structures

---

6.1 USING PARALLEL STRUCTURES

In English classes, you may have studied and practiced how to create parallel structures, including how to correct ones that were not parallel. Parallelism refers to two or more structures that have the same form, whether they be words, phrases, or clauses, and that serve the same function in a sentence, as in:

> Revising and editing were emphasized in my last writing class.

The structures *revising* and *editing* are parallel structures since they are both *-ing* nouns that function as subjects for this sentence. Writers use parallel structures to show how ideas are related and to focus on important ideas. These structures are especially useful in long sentences to help readers process information more easily, as in these examples from COCA.

> <u>Because</u> cloud providers use large, modern, efficient data centers, and <u>because</u> they share infrastructure among multiple companies, their costs to run the small part of the center a company is using are much lower than the costs would be for a server in its own data center.

> Helping patients to understand the effect of behavior on their health is imperative. For change to occur, they must believe <u>that</u> their behavior makes them vulnerable to a particular health problem, <u>that</u> the problem is potentially serious, and <u>that</u> the benefits of taking action outweigh the potential costs

Raising Language Awareness

Exercise 1

Each of the sentence pairs has one sentence that uses parallel structures with the same grammatical forms correctly and one sentence in which joined structures are not parallel. For each pair, write OK in the blank next to the sentence that uses parallel structures. The first one has been done for you as an example.

1. _OK_ a. A daydream can be defined as a fantasy indulged in while awake or as a wishful plan about the future.

_____ b. A daydream can be defined as a fantasy indulged in while awake or a person has a wishful plan about the future.

2. _____ a. Some psychologists have regarded extensive daydreaming as a symptom of unhappiness or even neurotic.

_____ b. Some psychologists have regarded extensive daydreaming as a symptom of unhappiness or even neurosis.

3. _____ a. However, psychologist Scott Barry Kaufman believes that certain kinds of daydreaming have many benefits and not always to be viewed negatively.

_____ b. However, psychologist Scott Barry Kaufman believes that certain kinds of daydreaming have many benefits and that daydreaming should not always be viewed negatively.

4. _____ a. Kaufman points out that daydreaming can help people reflect on their lives, plan their futures, develop creativity, or even amuse themselves in boring situations, such as being stuck in a traffic jam.

   _____ b. Kaufman points out that daydreaming can help people reflect on their lives, plan their futures, develop creativity, or even amusing themselves in boring situations, such as being stuck in a traffic jam.

5. _____ a. According to Kaufman, people who have not only the most positively oriented daydreams but also the most specific ones paradoxically score high in mindfulness, which involves attention control, mental flexibility, and other positive cognitive traits.

   _____ b. According to Kaufman, people who have not only the most positively oriented daydreams but they also have the most specific ones paradoxically score high in mindfulness, which involves attention control, being mentally flexible, and other positive cognitive traits.

Exercise 2

Read these sentences about the nature of happiness. The connectors that join parallel structures have been circled. For each sentence, put brackets around the parallel grammatical structures. A sentence may have more than one set. The first one has been done for you as an example.

_____ 1. Current research on what makes people happy has added [some fresh ideas] (as well as) [new insights] into this topic.

_____ 2. Scientists have looked at what happy people have in common (in addition to) why it's worth trying to become one of them.

_____ 3. Researchers have found that for many people happiness primarily results (not) from pursuing passive, pleasure-oriented activities (but) from striving toward excellence based on one's unique talents.

_____ 4. Psychologist David Schkade believes that people (neither) think often enough about how they spend their time (nor) consider how much of it they actually enjoy.

_____ 5. To increase a sense of happiness, Schkade recommends that people add to their daily lives something they enjoy doing, like spending time with friends, (or) that they take positive action to change something negative, such as improving their study habits.

_____ 6. If people are willing to analyze their current circumstances, which isn't always easy, (and) if they can question some of their long-held assumptions about what constitutes genuine happiness, they will have a better chance of making their lives more fulfilling (and) being truly content.

Building Your Knowledge

Purposes and Types of Parallel Structures

The use of parallel structures in writing has often been treated as a matter of grammatical correctness. Writing handbooks and internet sites warn that **faulty parallelism** is a type of writing error that requires editing. From this perspective, your task is to identify the faulty parallelism and then express the ideas using the same grammatical form.

We can also view parallel structures as a **language resource** for writers to craft elegant and effective sentences. From this perspective, parallelism can serve these purposes:

- to show how two or more ideas have equal importance

- to focus readers on important ideas (e.g., through *not only . . . but also* structures)

- to create rhythm and flow in a piece of writing, influencing how readers may either pause or move forward as they progress.

In short, when used well, parallel structures can help make ideas clear through balance, focus, and emphasis, and make your expression of the ideas more elegant.

Within sentences, the elements that can be made parallel fall into three broad categories: words, phrases, and clauses (see Table 6.1). In addition, a variety of connecting words and phrases link parallel structures. Common connecting words and phrases include conjunctions, addition connectors, and comparison words, as shown in Table 6.2.

Table 6.1: Types of Parallel Structures

Structures	Examples	Notes

Words (e.g., nouns, verbs, adjectives, and their modifiers)	1. Well-being involves striving for
	                                        noun
	    excellence based on <u>one's unique</u> <u>talents</u>
	    noun
	    and <u>potential</u>.
	                                  adjective
	 2. Happy people tend to be both <u>realistic</u>
	    adjective
	    and <u>open</u> to new things.
		When you join parts of speech, they do not need the same types or numbers of modifiers. In 1, *talents* has a modifier, but *potential* does not; in 2, *open* has a complement, but *realistic* does not.

Phrases (e.g., gerund phrases, infinitive phrases, and prepositional phrases)	3. With a good friend, you can enjoy
	                       gerund phrase
	    simple activities such as <u>listening to</u>
	               gerund phrase
	    <u>music</u> or <u>going to the movies together</u>.
	 4. People tend to get more enjoyment
	           prepositional phrase
	    <u>from spending time with close friends</u>
	           prepositional phrase
	    than <u>from chatting with acquaintances</u>.
		If a phrase is short, sometimes an introducer word such as a preposition does not need to be repeated for the second phrase—e.g., *You can make your life more interesting <u>by joining a club or trying a new sport</u>.*

Clauses (e.g., *that*-clauses, relative clauses, and adverb clauses)	**relative clause**
	 5. Those <u>who can analyze their life</u>
	            relative clause
	    <u>circumstances</u> and (<u>who can</u>) <u>take</u>
	
	    <u>positive action</u> are more likely to be
	
	    happy.
	 6. People achieve happiness not necessarily
	          adverb clause
	    <u>because they engage in activities</u>
	
	    <u>offering instant pleasure</u> but
	          adverb clause
	    <u>because they try to achieve their full</u>
	
	    <u>potential</u>.
		In 5, we could delete the second relative pronoun *who* and modal *can*.
		
		 However, in 6, deleting the second adverbial conjunction *because* and *they* would make the sentence ungrammatical since the sentence expresses a contrast (not X but Y).

While it's not necessary to know all the grammatical terms for these connectors, you should be able to recognize them in your writing so you can check to be sure the structures they join are the same kinds of grammatical elements.

Table 6.2: Common Connectors Signaling Parallel Structures

Kinds of Connectors	Examples
coordinating conjunctions	*and, but, or, nor, yet*
correlative conjunctions	*either … or, not only … but also, both …. and*
other addition connectors	*in addition to, as well as*
comparison words	*more… than, as… as*

Exercise 3

Complete each sentence with a parallel structure, repeating the underlined word or phrase and adding an idea that makes sense for the context. The first one has been done for you as an example.

1. Airplane flights are often delayed due <u>to</u> mechanical problems that get detected shortly before the scheduled departure or <u>to</u> <u>bad weather conditions such as fog or thunderstorms</u> .

2. A good leader is someone <u>who</u> has well-developed persuasive skills and _____

   _____ .

3. You can become a better academic writer <u>by</u> expanding your range of vocabulary and _____

   _____ .

4. College students often have part-time jobs <u>because </u>they need extra income or _____

   _____ .

5. To improve your study habits, I would recommend <u>that</u> you spend some time every day reviewing the lecture notes from your classes and _____ .

6.2 RECOGNIZING WORDS THAT INTRODUCE PARALLEL STRUCTURES

Just as it isn't essential to know the grammar terminology for the various connectors in order to use them effectively, it's not necessary to grammatically label every kind of word, phrase, or clause that is connected. To create and check for parallel structures, you do, however, need to be able to recognize words that fall into grammatical categories related to parts of speech, such as nouns, verbs, adverbs, adjectives, and prepositions and words that mark phrase and clause structures.

Raising Language Awareness

Exercise 4

Each sentence contains parallel structures. The connectors are circled and the first structure is shown in brackets. If a sentence is correct, write C in the blank provided. If it is incorrect due to faulty parallelism, write I in the blank. The first one has been done for you as an example.

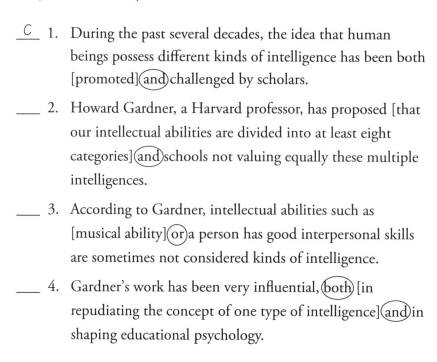

_C_ 1. During the past several decades, the idea that human beings possess different kinds of intelligence has been both [promoted] (and) challenged by scholars.

___ 2. Howard Gardner, a Harvard professor, has proposed [that our intellectual abilities are divided into at least eight categories] (and) schools not valuing equally these multiple intelligences.

___ 3. According to Gardner, intellectual abilities such as [musical ability] (or) a person has good interpersonal skills are sometimes not considered kinds of intelligence.

___ 4. Gardner's work has been very influential, (both) [in repudiating the concept of one type of intelligence] (and) in shaping educational psychology.

___ 5. Other scientists, however, argue that while the theory of multiple intelligences sounds nice, it is (more) [intuition] (than) empirical.

___ 6. Psychologist Lynn Waterhouse contends that multiple intelligence theory has little value for [clinical testing of intelligence] (or) to predict future performance.

___ 7. Behavioral scientist Christopher Ferguson points out that too many people believe in [what they wish to be true] (instead of) what the truth actually is.

___ 8. While Ferguson challenges the idea of multiple intelligences, he says we must avoid the fallacy [that some people deserve to live in poverty] (or) entire groups of people being inferior in respect to intelligence.

___ 9. Ferguson notes that in the past such fallacies have been used to justify [oppression] (and) racist.

___10. While he does not support the theory of multiple intelligenes, Ferguson agrees that [identifying strong and weak areas of achievement] (as well as) encourage exploration of talents are worthwhile pursuits.

Building Your Knowledge

As you evaluated the sentences in Exercise 4, you most likely drew on your knowledge of a variety of grammar structures. Recognizing words or parts of words that indicate grammatical categories and identifying those words that introduce phrases or clauses help you to create and check structures.

For example, it helps to know that many abstract nouns have endings such as *–ment, -ness,* or *–tion* (*investment, happiness, attention*) and that many *–ing* words, called gerunds, also function as nouns (*writing, researching, dancing*). It is useful to know that many single word adverbs are created by adding *–ly* to an adjective form (*elegantly, methodically, stubbornly*). When checking parallel prepositional phrases, it helps to know the words that function as prepositions such as *by, in, to,* or *with.*

For phrases other than prepositional phrases and for clauses, you want to be able to identify quickly the words that signal what kinds of structures need to be parallel:

- *what* and *how* often begin noun clauses (*what we need, how we think*)

- *who* and *which* are two words for relative clauses (*who told us, which is transformed*)

- *to* + verb can be an infinitive phrase or start an infinitive clause (*to perform, to find a cure*)

- words like *although* and *if* introduce adverb clauses (*if we have doubts, although it seems reasonable*) or sometimes precede reduced adverb clauses followed by participles (*although injured and exhausted*).

Parallel structures are frequently used in academic writing as well as in other kinds of writing. Consider the second sentence from the beginning of the explanation on page 118.

> Recognizing words or parts of words that indicate grammatical categories and identifying words that introduce phrases or clauses help you to create and check structures.

This sentence has four parallel structures, two of which are inside larger parallel structures.

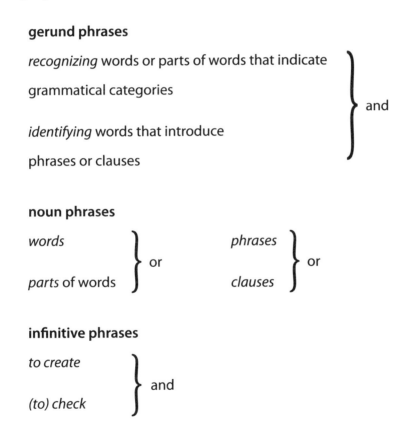

gerund phrases

recognizing words or parts of words that indicate grammatical categories

and

identifying words that introduce phrases or clauses

noun phrases

words

parts of words

or

phrases

clauses

or

infinitive phrases

to create

(to) check

and

As mentioned in Table 6.1, writers can omit phrase or clause introducers if they are the same as those that introduced previous phrases or clauses. For example, we did not have to repeat *to* for the second infinitive phrase. These omissions are a kind of **ellipsis**; that is, the reader can fill in the missing word or words from what has been written before. There are also cases where repeating phrase or clause marker words can improve rhythm and flow.

Table 6.3 offers some words and phrases to use when creating parallel structures and to keep in mind when checking for parallelism. It provides more specific vocabulary for the word and phrase types explained in Table 6.1.

Table 6.3: Common Phrase and Clause Introducers in Academic Writing

Type of Introducer	Examples	Phrase/Clause Examples
Preposition	*at, about, by, for, from, given, in, out, to, toward, with*	*for a good cause* *with sound principles*
Compound preposition	*according to, because of, due to, in respect to, on account of, with regard to*	*according to the evidence* *with regard to both issues*
Negative or quantifier word + preposition/ compound preposition	*not about, not because of, partly due to*	*not because of the distance* *partly due to other circumstances*
Relative pronoun	*who, that, which, whom, whose*	*the problem that arises* *the people whose lives are at stake*
Relative adverb	*when, where*	*the year when he was born* *the place where you should look for the answer*
Noun clause *wh*-word	*what, how, when*	*what the outcome will be* *when the answer is known*
***That*-complements**	*that*	*they announced that the election was over*
Infinitive	*to* + verb	*to investigate* *to consider the consequences of our actions*
Adverbial (subordinating) conjunction	*although, before, if, since, until, while, whereas*	*before we rush to a decision* *whereas the second proposal seems more feasible*

Exercise 5

Skim these sentences from "The Creative Personality" by Mihaly Csikszentmihalyi to get a sense of the main ideas. Put brackets around the parallel words, phrases, or clauses. Then underline any introducer words that tell you what kinds of structures are parallel. The first one has been done for you as an example.

1. Most of the things that are [interesting], [important], and [human] are the result of creativity.

2. But creativity also leaves an outcome that adds to the richness and complexity of the future.

3. Creative individuals are remarkable for their ability to adapt to almost any situation and to make do with whatever is at hand to reach their goals.

4. It seems that their energy is internally generated, due more to their focused minds than to the superiority of their genes.

5. This does not mean that creative people are hyperactive. In fact, they rest often and sleep a lot.

6. Creative people combine playfulness and discipline, or responsibility and irresponsibility.

7. Creative people tend to be both extroverted and introverted.

8. We are usually one or the other, preferring to be in the thick of crowds or sitting on the sidelines and observing the passing show.

Checking for Faulty Parallelism

Sometimes it is difficult to see at a glance what structures need to be parallel in a sentence. Follow these steps to identify and create parallel structures when revising.

1. Find and circle words or phrases that join structures: *and, but, or, as well as, not only…but also, either…or*, etc.

   > This report states that productivity in the United States has increased (but) real wages of Americans have fallen during the past decade.

2. Make ideas on each side of the circled word(s) parallel—that is, grammatically the same. First, get a sense of what ideas are parallel by carefully reading the entire sentence. Then, find the idea to the left of the circled word(s) and put brackets around it. If the parallel ideas are at the end of a sentence, the first part often is some type of structure right after the main verb.

   > This report states [that productivity in the United States has increased] (but) real wages of Americans have fallen during the past decade.

3. Find the parallel idea to the right of the circled word(s) and put brackets around it.

   > This report states that productivity in the United States has increased (but) [real wages of Americans have fallen during the past decade].

4. Compare the two bracketed parts. Pay special attention to the beginnings of the parts. Check to see if the first part begins with any phrase or clause introducers such as *that, who, to* + verb, etc. If not, determine if the first part is a noun phrase, a verb phrase, or some other structure.

> 1ˢᵗ part: [that productivity in the United States has increased]
>
> 2ⁿᵈ part: [real wages of Americans have fallen during the last decade]

The first bracketed part begins with a *that*-clause but the second one does not.

5. Revise your sentence to make the second part grammatically the same as the first part.

> This report states that productivity in the United States has increased but that real wages of Americans have fallen during the last decade.

Exercise 6

Identify the faulty parallelism and revise each sentence to make it grammatical and improve clarity. Use the circling and bracketing strategies to help you identify structures. The first one has been done for you as an example.

1. A recent study on sleep habits reports [that more than half of all Americans do not sleep well most nights] (and) [defining what constitutes insomnia is not an easy task].

   A recent study on sleep habits reports that more than half of

   all Americans do not sleep well most nights and that defining

   what constitutes insomnia is not an easy task.

2. People may complain about difficulty falling asleep or they wake up during the night.

   _____

   _____

3. Sleep research reveals that insomniacs almost always overestimate how long it took them to fall asleep and underestimating how long they actually slept.

   _____

   _____

   _____

4. For some with sleep difficulties, the problem lies in poor "sleep hygiene," or bad habits, such as they overconsume caffeine drinks or watching television in bed.

   _____

   _____

   _____

5. In past centuries, Western society slept in two shifts; people went to sleep, got up in the middle of the night for an hour or so, and then back to sleep.

   _____

   _____

   _____

6. Thus, according to history professor A. Roger Ekirch, some sleep disorders, namely waking up in the middle of night and unable to fall asleep again, may actually be a traditional pattern.

   _____

   _____

   _____

7. Anthropologist Carol Worthman notes that in our culture, quality sleep involves going into a dark and quiet room, falling asleep, do that for eight hours and then get up again.

   _____

   _____

   _____

8. Worthman points out that this 8-hour sleep model is not typical and science has never investigated empirically whether this way of sleeping has more benefits.

   _____

   _____

   _____

6.3 EMPHASIZING IDEAS WITH CORRELATIVE CONJUNCTIONS

Raising Language Awareness

Correlative conjunctions are used to join many types of parallel structures. These connectors are a more complex form of coordination than the simple coordinators such as *and, or,* and *but* since they occur in pairs. The most common correlative conjunctions in English are

> *both … and*
> *either … or*
> *neither … nor*
> *not only … but also*

In writing guides, the discussion of correlative conjunctions tends to focus on rules of subject-verb agreement when they are used to connect subject noun phrases. For example, **the proximity rule** states that the verb should agree with the number of the noun phrase closest to it:

> Neither *the members of Congress* nor <u>*the President*</u> has left the Capitol building yet.

However, note that correlative conjunctions are often used both to emphasize the words and phrases that follow them and to allow writers to express ideas more concisely and elegantly. For example, in the previous sentence, the ideas joined by correlative conjunctions *both…and* could have been written as separate sentences:

> Correlative conjunctions are often used to emphasize the words and phrases that follow them.

> They allow writers to express ideas more concisely and elegantly.

In sum, conjunction pairs serve both functional (emphasis) and stylistic purposes in ways that simple conjunctions do not. They are especially useful in complex sentences when the parts that are joined are more than just a word or simple phrase, as shown in some of the examples taken from academic texts in this section.

Exercise 7

Circle the correlative conjunctions and put brackets around the parallel structures they connect. Passages may have more than one pair of correlative conjunctions. The first one has been done for you as an example.

1. The connection between water scarcity and pollution can lead to problems of water access…. Water scarcity (not only) [makes it more difficult to get adequate and clean water to meet human needs], (but also) [harms aquatic habitats and species downstream].

2. The literature on parent involvement in children's sports tends to focus on either negative or positive outcomes. It seems important to point out that parent involvement in their child's sport experiences is inherently neither good nor bad.

3. Business should not feel the need to overstep its boundaries or take on responsibilities that belong to the state. Companies that practice global corporate citizenship do so either through thought leadership, that is providing the knowledge and technology essential to addressing a global problem, or through concrete action, that is through the execution of a coordinated plan.

4. There is much to explore about the functional anatomy of talent. Why talent? It is a concept broad enough to encompass questions related to both intelligence and creativity.

5. It is incorrect to say that the state of violence currently in Iraq is due to U.S. actions alone, and not due to any pre-existing conditions created by the former regime. The march towards some form of democratic governance will flow neither from the barrel of a gun nor from the slot of a ballot box.

6. Understanding the nature of graphic communication—a form of communication that is both atemporal and spatial—forms a key foundation for communicating scientific and technical information. It is essential for graphic design students to understand why and how to effectively transform data into graphics to both engage the viewer and communicate information.

Building Your Knowledge

Correlative conjunctions are used quite frequently in academic writing in order to place special emphasis on ideas. In fact, some correlative conjunctions are not often used outside of formal writing or speaking contexts. Although speakers may sometimes use these connectors in informal speech, they often don't pay much attention to making the connected ideas grammatically parallel.

Most of the correlative conjunctions emphasize the equal status of the two joined ideas.

> New research has linked insufficient sleep to both poorer metabolism and appetite control.

However, the conjunction pair *not only… but also* allows us to emphasize the second of two ideas.

> *New research has linked insufficient sleep not only to poorer metabolism but also to appetite control.*

With *but also,* the writer signals that the reader should pay more attention to the second idea. In some cases, the idea is one that the writer believes may be surprising to readers.

Subject-Verb Inversion with *not only… (but) also*

When you join two independent clauses with the conjunctions *not only… (but) also*, invert the subject and the first verb or auxiliary verb of the clause after *not only.*

> Clause 1: Due to domestication, dogs can communicate feelings to humans.
>
> Clause 2: Dogs can also read human cues such as body posture.
>
> Combined: Due to domestication, not only <u>can dogs communicate</u> feelings to humans, but they can also read human cues such as body posture.

Note that *can* comes between *but* and *also* in the second clause. While it would not be incorrect to write *but also they can read...,* placement after the auxiliary verb is the most typical word order. One other thing to note is that writers often omit either *but* or *also* when they are joining ideas expressed in two clauses.

Not only can dogs communicate feelings to humans $\Big\}$ but *they can read....*

they can also *read....*

If the auxiliary verb is the same in both clauses, you also have the option of placing the *not only* conjunction after the first auxiliary and deleting the second one. Because only verb phrases and not clauses are joined, there is no inversion needed.

> Dogs can not only communicate feelings to humans but read human cues such as body posture.

In cases where there is no auxiliary verb such as a *be* verb or a modal verb, some form of *do* needs to be placed before *not only*:

> Dogs communicate feelings to human and read human cues such as body posture. →

> Not only *do* dogs communicate feelings to human but they also read human cues.

To decide which forms to choose and where to place the conjunctions, consider:

- types of ideas you are connecting
- what idea(s) you want to emphasize
- conciseness
- elegance (that is, the resulting sentence rhythm).

Exercise 8

Each sentence has parallel forms joined by the coordinating conjunctions *and*, *but*, or *so*. Substitute the appropriate correlative conjunctions in each sentence to emphasize one or more joined structures. Make any other changes necessary. Try to use a variety of correlative conjunctions. The first one has been done for you as an example.

1. Some dogs learn to understand hundreds of words and remember them for a period of time.

   Some dogs not only learn to understand hundreds of words but also remember them for a period of time.

2. Although dogs can imitate human speech, such as the words "I love you," they cannot actually talk and they do not understand full sentences the way we do. (*Hint*: Consider using *neither/nor* and changing the negative verbs *cannot* and *do not* to positive verbs.)

   _____

   _____

   _____

3. Psychologist Gary Lucas says that the vocal imitation skills of dogs are quite limited, so the sounds need to be shaped by selective attention and behavioral rewards such as treats.

   _____

   _____

   _____

4. Dogs can indicate meaning through intensity or duration of their vocalizations.

   _____

   _____

5. A dog's tail wag could express happiness, but in some situations might signal a state of anxiety.

   _____

   _____

6. Dogs bark to express a variety of emotions, such as loneliness, fear, or pleasure, and to show desire for an activity such as getting food or fetching a ball.

   _____

   _____

7. Cats have a variety of vocalizations, including purring, meowing, and hissing, and a range of body language, such as tail twitching, head bumping, and yawning, to express themselves.

   _____

   _____

   _____

8. Careers in animal training can be exciting and financially rewarding.

   _____

   _____

9. Some animal training careers, such as for marine animals, require a high school diploma and a bachelor's degree in a special field.

   _____

   _____

10. Animal trainers must be patient and sensitive and should have experience with problem-solving and animal obedience.

    _____

    _____

Part 2: Connecting and Focusing across Sentences

Chapter 7: Creating Cohesion with Word Forms and Reference Words and Phrases

Chapter 6 explored the ways that writers can connect ideas between words, phrases, and clauses in sentences by using coordinating conjunctions (e.g., *and*, *or*) as well as correlative conjunctions (e.g., *both…and, either…or*).

This chapter examines how writers can make connections and create cohesion across sentences. In making these kinds of connections, vocabulary plays an important role. To create links, writers use a variety of strategies that make reference to vocabulary previously used. This strategy could involve word repetition or the use of a different form of a previously used word (e.g., *reduce* in one sentence followed by *reduction* in another sentence). Or the connection may involve the use of a classifier, or summary, noun. Classifier nouns are extremely useful because they can refer back to large sections of a text. For example, to refer back several paragraphs, or even pages, discussing the ways in which one solution is better than another for a particular situation, a writer might use *these advantages*. To make the lexical (vocabulary) links even clearer, writers use reference words like *this* or *these* to modify repeated words, word forms, or classifier nouns.

Raising Language Awareness

Exercise 1

Each passage taken from COCA illustrates a way that writers can create cohesion across sentences. Circle each word or phrase in each passage that repeats, echoes, or connects to the idea(s) expressed by the underlined phrase(s) in the previous sentence(s). The first one has been done for you as an example.

1. Topic: Shortage of math teachers

   Santa Cruz–based Center for the Future of Teaching and Learning slapped a strongly worded warning label on the state's new algebra requirement, saying <u>the state doesn't have nearly enough qualified teachers to do the job</u>. "Scant attention has been paid to this critical issue, and California's approach to math instruction still doesn't add up," according to the Center's July report on the issue.

2. Topic: Teaching method changes

   If teachers want to bring changes into their teaching methods for the solution of problems and the establishment of their own theories, they should make an effort to <u>improve their teaching methods</u>. However, the improvement of teaching methods cannot be made within a short period of time. Teachers should frequently take part in a supervision process and share their ideas and reflections with other teachers.

3. Topic: Publishing plastic surgery research

   <u>The present analysis</u> will serve as a first step in evaluating the effectiveness with which plastic surgeons publish novel information first presented in abstract form. It will also estimate time requirements for successful research publications and determine which plastic surgery journals are final destinations for presented abstracts.

4. Topic: Predictors of athletic performance

   [It was believed that] (a) psychological skill would predict subjective athletic performance, (b) self-confidence would be the single strongest predictor of performance, and (c) sex of athlete and type of sport would significantly predict performance. While these hypotheses were generally confirmed, it was also observed that some of the significant psychological skills predicted performance in a negative direction (e.g., coachability and goal setting).

5. Topic: Academy of Motion Pictures Arts and Sciences

   They're out of tune with the times. They're swayed by the emotional rather than the cerebral. They go for the familiar and reassuring over the innovative and challenging. Members of Congress? American Idol judges? Nope. Try the Academy of Motion Picture Arts and Sciences, the organization that for 83 years has been handing out Oscars for outstanding achievements in the film industry. Such accusations routinely are hurled by those in the entertainment media and movie lovers who watch at home as they question the choices of the 5,755-member group that decides who wins those coveted gold statuettes.

6. Topic: Effects of sleep deprivation on health

   Good reasons to get more shut-eye—you'll live longer. Chronic insomniacs are more likely to suffer a heart attack than those who sleep well, according to new research in the journal *Circulation*. Other studies have linked lack of sleep to a higher risk of dying from a stroke and developing breast cancer.

7.1 USING WORD FORMS TO CONNECT IDEAS

Raising Language Awareness

One way to create cohesion is to echo ideas through use of different word forms or derivatives. These lists of words present different word derivatives or word families.

1. analytical, analytically, analysis, analyze, reanalyze
2. insignificant, significance, significant, significantly, signify
3. distinct, distinctive, distinctly, distinction, indistinct
4. invalid, invalidate, valid, validate, validity
5. predict, predictable, predictably, prediction, unpredictability, unpredictable
6. intense, intensely, intensify, intensity, intensive

Exercise 2

Place each word from the list into its proper place in the chart based on part of speech. There may be more than one answer in any one cell. The first one has been done for you as an example.

	Noun	Verb	Adjective	Adverb
1	analysis	analyze reanalyze	analytical	analytically
2				
3				
4				
5				
6				

Building Your Knowledge

For readers, a key to following the ideas in complex passages is understanding the words and phrases that create links between sentences. Toward the beginning of a new sentence or paragraph, a writer can repeat information from a previous sentence or paragraph by using different word forms to create lexical chains.

1. According to Jared Diamond in *Guns, Germs, and Steel,* societies <u>tend</u> to reject or adopt new technologies for many reasons.

2. Some <u>tendencies</u> may seem illogical at first glance.

The writer builds cohesion by using the word forms *tend* in Sentence 1 and *tendencies* in Sentence 2 to create a link.

Exercise 3

Read these paragraphs about technological advances. For each numbered and underlined word or phrase, use a different form of the word(s) in the like-numbered blank later in the passage to echo ideas and build cohesion.

According to Jared Diamond, many new inventions are never (4) adopted by society. Diamond notes that, while many inventions are more (1) efficient than older technologies, (1) _____is not always the main factor in embracing a new technology. Often, a society has economic reasons for holding on to an older technology and thus (2) rejects the new one. For example, the (2) _____ of electric lighting in England can be traced to massive investments in gas lighting. In addition, some ancient Mexican societies never adopted the wheel for transportation, as they (3) were not able to use animals to pull wheeled vehicles. This (3)_____ to use animals rendered wheeled vehicles useless and thus uneconomical.

Another factor affecting the (4) _____ of new technologies is (5) resistance to (6) change. In the 1930s, typists (5)_____ the introduction of a new, more efficient typewriter keyboard given that typists were used to the old keyboard and did not want to (6)_____ their habits. Often a new item is adopted or rejected based not on its use or economic value but on its social (7) value. One such example is expensive designer jeans, which are more highly (7)_____ than cheaper generic jeans. Another example is the (8) preference of Japan's *kanji* writing system over the *kana* system. Many people (8)_____ using *kanji*, even though it is a quite difficult system, because it holds social prestige.

7.2 USING REFERENCE FORMS

Raising Language Awareness

Reference forms are also important in creating links between ideas. Exercise 4 will help you identify different reference forms.

Exercise 4

Decide which one of these sentences is the better choice to follow the first sentence. Be ready to explain your choice.

Many countries have laws that require children to get some kind of education.

a. *They* differ in the number of years education is mandatory

b. *These laws* differ in the number of years education is mandatory.

For each sentence pair, circle the words or phrases in Sentence B that refer to something in Sentence A. Put brackets around the words or phrases in Sentence A that are being referred to or expanded. There may be more than one referent in Sentence B. The first one has been done for you as an example.

1. A. [Childhood] is a term that usually refers to the human developmental period between infancy and adulthood.

   B. In psychology, (it) is typically divided into several stages.

2. A. Early childhood comes after infancy.

   B. This stage begins when a child starts speaking or walking and ends around the age of seven or eight.

3. A. Cultures vary as to when they determine a child becomes an adult.

   B. Such variation results from differences in the age at which cultures consider a person mature enough to have certain rights or responsibilities.

4. A. Many historians have researched social attitudes toward childhood over the centuries.

 B. This research reveals that the concept of childhood has changed dramatically over time in many cultures.

5. A. All U.S. states have laws requiring a period of educational attendance for children.

 B. Most of these laws, known as compulsory education, allow home schooling.

6. A. The ages for which education is required vary from state to state.

 B. For example, the range is between 5 and 16 in Maryland; in Ohio it is between 6 and 18, and in Washington between 8 and 17.

7. A. One benefit of compulsory education worldwide is that it has discouraged child labor.

 B. Another is that it helps to prepare individuals for vocations and professions in adulthood.

8. A. Our current system of compulsory education does, however, have its critics; one objection to mandatory schooling is that it stifles creativity.

 B. Others include the beliefs that not all individuals are suited for schooling and that compulsory education interferes with individual liberty.

Building Your Knowledge

Using Reference Forms to Connect and Focus

Often occurring with reference words such as *the* or *this* are noun phrases that refer back to previous ideas to make explicit connections between ideas. In academic writing, these reference words often occur with words that function as **classifiers**, words such as *idea, issue, problem,* or *factor*. (See a more complete list in the Appendix.)

Reference forms and examples in English are listed in Table 7.1. The demonstrative determiners *this, that, these,* and *those* and comparative forms *another* and *the other* can also be used alone as pronouns.

This is an important issue; those are the main findings; another is the way children dress.

While sentence connector words such as *however, therefore,* or *in addition* are often used to show relationships, they are often not appropriate or sufficient to express the complex relationships that writers are working with in larger pieces of writing.

Table 7.1: Reference Forms with Classifier Nouns

Reference Form	Noun Phrase Examples
this	*this critical issue*
that	*that outdated notion*
these	*these two competing hypotheses*
those	*those considerations*
such	*such accusations*
the + noun phrase	*the first topic that was discussed*
another	*another important question*
other/the other	*other factors/the other concern*

Exercise 5

Each set of sentences is missing cohesive devices. In the blank, use one of the following constructions: *this* + singular noun or *these* + plural noun. Choose a noun form based on the underlined word(s) in the first sentence of each passage. The first one has been done for you as an example.

1. The company <u>mistakenly</u> published confidential client information on their website. <u>This mistake</u> may lead to identity theft and credit-rating problems for customers.

2. Scientists <u>warn</u> about the dangers caused by pollution— global warming, loss of ecological balance, health problems, and more. However, some people believe that, because _____ are not covered enough by the media, they go unheeded.

3. Some people <u>assume</u> that children are not reading enough and are becoming bad writers because of the increased use of the internet. According to recent studies, _____ have been proven false.

4. In his book *Outliers*, Malcolm Gladwell <u>theorizes</u> that practicing any task—from music to mathematics—for a total of approximately 10,000 hours will help a person achieve success. _____ has been criticized by sociologists, who believe that he oversimplifies complex phenomena.

5. In the U.S., it is <u>expected</u> that all children in elementary school should receive ninety minutes of music instruction per week. However, in many schools _____ is not being met, and experts worry that music appreciation will wane.

Using *such* vs. Demonstrative Determiners to Connect Ideas

The reference form *such* serves a very useful purpose in expressing ideas that link to previous ones. Its meaning differs from the demonstrative forms *this, that, these,* and *those.*

Consider these sentences:

Some college campuses have noted increasing rude behavior in classrooms, especially large lecture halls. For example, students carry on conversations among themselves while the professor is lecturing.

Now consider these two options that could follow and their explanations.

Options	Explanations
This behavior is creating an uncivil classroom environment.	*This* refers to the specific behavior of students talking during a lecture.
Such behavior is creating an uncivil classroom environment.	*Such* refers to behavior of this kind or type, in this case, rude or uncivil behavior. For example, in this context, *such behavior* could include texting.

Exercise 6

Underline the ideas to which the reference forms in Sentences A and B refer. Explain the difference in meaning between the sentences in each set.

1. In some lecture halls, students spend their time searching the web or answering e-mail on their laptops instead of paying attention to the lecture.

    A. These activities may distract the students around them.

    B. Such activities may distract the students around them.

    _____

    _____

    _____

2. Uncivil campus behavior can also be found in living spaces such as dormitories. For example, students may play loud music constantly in their dorm rooms.

    A. This situation makes it harder for those around them to study or even sleep.

    B. Such a situation makes it harder for those around them to study or even sleep.

    _____

    _____

    _____

Exercise 7

State the rules explaining which kinds of nouns need *such a* and which nouns require *such* without an article.

1. With singular count nouns, use _____

   _____.

2. With plural count nouns, use _____

   _____.

3. With non-count nouns, use _____

   _____.

Now create an example sentence for each rule. In each sentence, use the classifier from the Appendix.

1. _____

   _____

2. _____

   _____

3. _____

   _____

Exercise 8

Write a sentence using *such a/an* or *such* + a classifier noun phrase to follow each sentence. See the Appendix for a list of classifier nouns. The first one has been done for you as an example.

1. Road rage, in which motorists act rudely or even violently to other drivers, is another type of incivility in contemporary society. In some cases, drivers have even tried to run over people with whom they are angry.

   Such rude and criminal actions are shocking; they have led to articles calling for drivers to be more considerate and for society to deal severely with crimes resulting from road rage.

2. On most American college campuses, students must take a series of general education courses, including history, mathematics, science, literature, and others.

   _____

   _____

   _____

3. In April 2010, the Deepwater Horizon oil drilling mobile unit exploded in the Gulf Coast, causing one of the worst oil spills in history.

   _____

   _____

   _____

4. The ways in which cultures differ in their conversational styles have long interested language researchers. For example, in some cultures, when two people meet they must exchange information about their families' health, whereas this would not be a conversation topic in other cultures. As another example, the rules for taking turns in a conversation may differ in terms of when a person can interrupt another or how long a person should wait before beginning to speak.

_____

_____

_____

Checking Verb Agreement with Long Subjects

When creating subject noun phrases that link ideas across sentences, writers sometimes produce complex sentence subjects. Finding the noun for which the verb needs to agree in number, which we will call the **head noun**, is not always easy. Using strategies like bracketing the words that make up the complete subject and crossing out modifiers such as prepositional phrases in a long noun phrase subject are helpful. Here is an example adapted from the passage in Exercise 3.

> Another factor in considering how new technologies get adopted **is/are** resistance to change.

First, look for the verb that needs to agree. We want to know here if it should be _is_ or _are_. Next, move to the left of that verb to find what the complete subject is and put brackets around it:

> [Another factor in considering how new technologies get adopted] **is/are**

Then, cross out the prepositional phrase starting with _in._ This makes it easier to see that the singular noun _factor_—not the plural noun _technologies_—is the subject, making the correct verb singular _is:_

> [Another **factor** ~~in considering how new technologies get adopted~~] **is**/are resistance to change.

Exercise 9

For each sentence from a passage about childhood pressures, use the strategies explained to find the subject head noun that needs to agree with the verb. Find the verb and underline it. Put brackets around the whole noun phrase that is the subject. Then put a line through phrases that start with prepositions such as *of, in, on* and through any infinitive *to*-phrase modifiers. When you have identified the head noun, circle it. The first one has been done for you as an example.

1. [Today's (pressures) ~~on middle-class children to grow up fast~~] <u>begin</u> in early childhood.

2. The trend toward early academic pressure was further supported by the civil rights movement.

3. One consequence of all this concern for the early years was the demise of the "readiness" concept.

4. But the emphasis on early intervention and early stimulation (even of infants) made the concept of readiness appear dated and old-fashioned.

5. The pressure to engage in competitive sports is one of the most obvious pressures on contemporary children to grow up fast.

Exercise 10

Edit this paragraph for three subject-verb agreement errors. In each sentence, underline the main verb. In the subject phrase, cross out prepositional phrases. Then circle the head noun. If the number of the main verb is incorrect, cross out the verb and write the correct form above the verb. The first one has been done for you as an example.

(1) The Model Minority (myth) ~~in America~~ *introduces* ~~introduce~~ Asian Americans as a successful ethnic minority with higher median incomes than other groups. (2) These assertions of achievement for Asian Americans conceal many facts. (3) One of the facts concealed are that Asian-American families live disproportionately in high cost-of-living areas such as New York and Los Angeles. (4) An emphasis on this material success of Asian Americans also pervade the media's focus on their educational status at "the top of the class." (5) Contrary to these media reports, almost all of the academic studies on the actual returns from their education point to prevalent discrimination toward Asian Americans.

Using Comparative Reference Forms

In writing that involves listing and classifying, writers often use comparative reference forms. Some forms can be used as pronouns as well as before noun phrases, as shown in Table 7.2. Note how the adjective forms can be used with long noun phrases in case information needs to be repeated for clarity. Because these reference forms are so similar, it is easy to confuse them.

Table 7.2: Comparative Reference Forms

Comparative Form	Pronouns	Adjectives + Noun Phrases	Meaning and Usage Notes
another	One goal of this chapter is to familiarize writers with reference forms. **Another** is to provide practice with these forms.	**Another goal of this chapter** is to provide practice with reference forms.	Use when there may be more than two members of the category.
the + other	In 2015, there were two states in the U.S. with populations over 20 million. One was California. **The other** was Texas.	**The other state with a population over 20 million in 2015** was Texas.	Use when you are distinguishing two things in a category.
[number] + *other*	Fewer than ten states have populations under 1 million. Wyoming and Vermont are two of them. **One other** is Alaska.	**Three other states that currently have populations under 1 million** are Montana, South Dakota, and North Dakota.	The meaning of *one other* is similar to *another* but more specific; similarly, phrases with plural numbers + *other* are more specific than just *others*.
others (pronoun) *other* + plural noun phrase (adjective)	The state with the most people is California. **Others** with high populations are Florida, Illinois, and New York.	**Other states with high populations** are Georgia and Michigan.	These forms are specific in number, involving two or more items related to a category. When using *the other(s)* or *others*, it is important to remember to include *the* or the plural *–s* ending of *other* when needed.

Exercise 11

Fill in the blank with an appropriate comparative reference form. The first one has been done for you as an example.

1. As most everyone knows, one of the most popular social networking internet sites is Facebook. <u>Others</u> are LinkedIn, Tumblr, and Twitter.

2. For Twitter, whose brief messages up to 140 characters are called tweets, informational sites abound; for example, one site lists special vocabulary describing Twitter users and tweeting activities; _____ offers rules of tweeting etiquette.

3. A number of Twitter terms refer to users of Twitter. One is *tweeple*; _____ are *tweeps* and *tweeters*. _____, which describes people who tweet too much, is *tweeterboxes*.

4. Two more Twitter terms refer to tweeting overuse; one, *tweetaholism*, indicates an apparent addiction to tweeting; _____, *tweetacholic*, describes a person who seems to be addicted to Twitter.

Exercise 12

Underline the comparative reference form in the last sentence of each group and decide if the form is correct or incorrect. If the comparative reference is correct, put C in the blank. If it is incorrect, put I in the blank, cross it out, and write a correction. More than one correct form is possible. Explain why the incorrect forms are wrong. The first one has been done for you as an example.

__I__ 1. Genetically modified (GM) foods, which have had their DNA altered, have been on the market since the early 1990s. Today many kinds of GM foods are sold. Soybeans are one of the most common modified foods.
 Others
 ~~The others~~ are corn and strawberries.

Explanation: There are a number of genetically modified foods

other than soybeans. Corn and strawberries are only two

others.

____ 2. The first commercial whole food crop to be genetically altered was a kind of tomato. Other crop involved in early genetic engineering experiments was cotton.

_____

_____

_____

____ 3. The majority of GM crops are grown in the United States. However, it is not the only country producing GM foods. Some other include Argentina, Brazil, and China.

_____

_____

_____

___ 4. A number of advantages of GM foods have been proposed. One of the biggest advantages is that foods can be altered to resist pests and thus reduce the use of pesticides. Another is that plants can be altered to be more tolerant to cold temperatures.

___ 5. Many concerns have been voiced regarding GM foods. Critics have argued that our knowledge of genes and how they work is too incomplete to be aware of the consequences of modifying food. One critical concern is these foods could be unsafe for humans. Others concerns involve the risks to farmed ecosystems and to wildlife.

7.3 USING REFERENCE FORMS WITH THE PASSIVE

Raising Language Awareness

A concept that readers often use to describe how information in a piece of writing is easily understandable is **flow**. In other words, the reader can move from sentence to sentence with a clear understanding of how the ideas are connected. To achieve flow from sentence to sentence, writers need to consider how they order information to keep focus on their main topics.

Exercise 13

Read the A and B versions of each short passage. Identify the main topics, underline the parts in A and B that differ, and then explain which you think has better flow and how this has been achieved. The first one has been done for you as an example.

1. A. Most of us have at least a few bad habits, such as overeating or gossiping, that we would like to break. In most cases, <u>a person can associate a bad habit</u> with many different places or activities. As a result, that habit cannot be easily broken without a lot of willpower.

   B. Most of us have at least a few bad habits, such as overeating or gossiping, that we would like to break. In most cases, <u>a bad habit can be associated</u> with many different places or activities. As a result, that habit cannot be easily broken without a lot of willpower.

Main Topic: bad habits

Explanation: The B version flows better because in the second sentence "a bad habit" is in the subject position instead of "a person." "A person" is not the topic of the passage.

2. A. An urban legend is a form of modern folktale or story. Typically, these stories are circulated by word of mouth or e-mail, and they are sometimes repeated in news articles. Urban legends are not always completely false. However, any true elements have usually been distorted or exaggerated over time.

   B. An urban legend is a form of modern folktale or story. Typically, people circulate these stories by word of mouth and email, and news articles sometimes repeat them. Urban legends are not always completely false. However, any true elements have usually been distorted or exaggerated over time.

Main Topic: _____

Explanation: _____

_____

3. A. Soccer, one of the most popular sports throughout the world, has a long history. There is some evidence that a form of soccer was played in China during the second century BCE. However, soccer as played today originated in the early nineteenth century in England. The game was first played by the British aristocracy; later it was taken up by the other social classes.

   B. Soccer, one of the most popular sports throughout the world, has a long history. There is some evidence that people played a form of soccer in China during the second century BCE. However, soccer as played today originated in the early nineteenth century in England. The British aristocracy first played the game; later the other social classes took it up.

Main Topic: _____

Explanation: _____

_____

_____

Building Your Knowledge

One way that writers create cohesion, establish a flow of information across sentences, and help readers focus on their main topics is to put those topics in the subject position. In many kinds of academic writing, writers craft sentences in the passive voice to accomplish this. The persons performing an activity—scientists, researchers, or perhaps people in general—are not as important as the activity itself. See Table 7.3.

Table 7.3: Ways to Create Cohesion through Passive Sentences

a. **A lingua franca** is a language that is used for communication between people who do not speak the same mother tongue. **Such languages** <u>have been adopted</u> for communication in political, educational, and business settings.	The first sentence or sentences in a paragraph may introduce a topic using either active or passive voice. At least some subsequent sentences may be written in the passive voice to keep the topic as a grammatical subject.
b. **Classical Chinese** once served as a diplomatic language for much of Far East Asia. In the early 20th century, **this language** <u>was replaced</u> by modern written standard Mandarin within China. However, in some parts of China, **standard Cantonese and other languages** <u>are used</u> for communication between speakers of different dialects.	As a paragraph progresses, related topics may be introduced in the subject position, with verbs in passive voice as needed to maintain the topic focus. Note that reference words and classifier words, such as *this language* in (b), are often used for repeated topics.

Exercise 14

Rewrite the underlined sentences to create cohesion. To keep focus on the main topics, change active sentences to passive where needed and keep the verb tenses the same. The first one has been done for you as an example.

1. Sometimes for no apparent reason, the hard drive of a computer crashes. <u>Worn parts that no longer align correctly cause many hard drive failures.</u> Such misalignments make it impossible to read data from the drive.

   Many hard drive failures are caused by parts that no longer

   align correctly.

2. The European Union (EU) is a political and economic union of member states. <u>Independent sovereign states established it in 1993.</u> To join the EU, a country must meet what are known as the Copenhagen criteria. <u>The European Council determines fulfillment of these criteria.</u>

   _____

   _____

   _____

   _____

3. How do memories get formed and retained in the brain? According to researchers Robert Stickgold and Jeffrey Ellenbogen, when we encode information in our brain, the new memory is just embarking on what will be a long journey. <u>The brain stabilizes, enhances, and transforms the memory until it is quite different from its original form. The brain retains this resulting memory in a detailed form something like a story.</u>

_____

_____

_____

_____

4. California sea otters have been struggling to repopulate after being hunted almost to extinction in the early 20th century. Although these marine mammals have gained protection through their status as an endangered species, the health of the sea otter population continues to be threatened. <u>Polluted runoff has weakened their immune systems. And recently, an ancient microbe found in warmer waters has been poisoning them.</u> As a result of these threats, their numbers have been declining.

_____

_____

_____

_____

Chapter 8: Creating Cohesion with Topic Introducers and Logical Connectors

This chapter focuses on two sets of academic vocabulary: words and phrases that academic writers use to introduce topics and those that academic writers use to create logical connections between ideas. It also focuses on helping you build your academic vocabulary by providing practice with both abstract nouns in general and classifier nouns in particular (see the Appendix).

When linking ideas across sentences and paragraphs, writers may use words and phrases with reference forms that introduce their topics.

> Concerning the use of laptops in the classroom, both instructors and students expressed ambivalence.

> With respect to the question of laptop use, instructors listed both benefits and drawbacks.

Writers can also use logical connectors before reference forms to express relationships between previous topics and new ones.

> Due to the problems mentioned, the company changed its hiring policies.

> Based on these focus group results, the company changed the packaging of the new product.

> Similar to previous findings, this study also uncovered a relationship between diet and work productivity.

> In contrast to previous findings, adolescents in our study list quality of life, not economic security, as the most important element of an ideal career.

Raising Language Awareness

Exercise 1

Circle the topic introducer word or phrase in the last sentence of each passage adapted from COCA. Underline the words the writer is referring to in the preceding text. The first one has been done for you as an example.

1. A number of questions were raised regarding how grades were computed. An initial issue was <u>whether or not the department had a policy on grading</u>. The idea here was to get a sense of whether faculty members agreed on how such things as skill, knowledge, and class participation should be weighed in determining a student's performance. (In regard to) this question, 80% of respondents indicated that their departments did not have a formal grading policy.

2. As a result of the 1965 changes in the Immigration and Nationality Act emphasizing family reunification, the number of parents of U.S. citizens admitted annually doubled between 1980 and 1990. Related to this increase, from 1986 to 1996, the number of noncitizens receiving SSI benefits rose from slightly over 244,000 to almost 800,000.

3. FDA officials claim that past inefficiency and excesses have been remedied and that the time required for approval of drugs for marketing is shrinking. Contrary to these assertions, in recent years the FDA has arguably moved in the opposite direction, introducing numerous obstacles to drug manufacture and clinical testing.

4. In Latin America during the 1970s, when the school-age population expanded dramatically, public spending per primary-school student fell by 45% in real terms. In Mexico, life expectancy for the poorest 10% of the population is 20 years less than for the richest 10%. Based on such analyses, the World Bank has stated: "The evidence points overwhelmingly to the conclusion that population growth at the rates common in most of the developing world slows development."

5. Alas, our economic forecasts call for rising pricing pressures and a steady federal funds rate. In short, investors may be disappointed if the Fed doesn't cut rates anytime soon—and we don't think it will. Given these trends and outlooks, we recently signaled to our investor clients that they should consider paring back the exposure to stocks in their portfolios.

6. In Iowa, land values jumped nearly 45 percent from 1986 to 1989, though they're still far below 1981 peak levels. Less than one in five farmers had significant money troubles last year, compared with a third in 1986.... In Minnesota, state officials say soil moisture is the best it has been since November 1986. Despite such optimistic signs, drought persists in areas, including Florida and parts of Colorado.

8.1: USING TOPIC INTRODUCERS WITH REFERENCE FORMS TO CONNECT IDEAS

Building Your Knowledge

Words and phrases like *concerning, regarding,* or *in reference to* signal a topic is "about" something; they are called **topic introducers.** When topic introducers are followed by reference forms with nouns, they signal how a new topic connects with what has been discussed in previous sentences or paragraphs. An example from Exercise 1 shows how topic introducers help build cohesion for the reader. Compare this example written with and without a topic introducer.

Without a Topic Introducer	With a Topic Introducer
A number of questions were raised regarding how grades were computed. An initial issue was whether or not the department had a policy on grading. The idea here was to get a sense of whether faculty members agreed on how such things as skill, knowledge, and class participation should be weighed in determining a student's performance. 80% of respondents indicated that their departments did not have a formal grading policy.	A number of questions were raised regarding how grades were computed. An initial issue was <u>whether or not the department had a policy on grading.</u> The idea here was to get a sense of whether faculty members agreed on how such things as skill, knowledge, and class participation should be weighed in determining a student's performance. *In regard to this question,* 80% of respondents indicated that their departments did not have a formal grading policy.

The third sentence refers back to the initial issue established in the first sentence: *whether or not the department had a policy on grading.* The second sentence adds information about the initial issue, which is important, but it interrupts the connection between the first and last sentences. By adding a topic introducer, this writer makes that connection explicit. Such explicit connections are a characteristic of good academic writing, whether the writer is connecting ideas across sentences or paragraphs.

Table 8.1: Topic Introducers and Examples

Topic Introducers	Examples with Reference Forms
as for	*As for the first question*
concerning	*Concerning this ongoing problem*
related to	*Related to the second suggestion*
in regard to	*In regard to the first finding*
regarding	*Regarding such assertions*
with reference to*	*With reference to the third solution I have proposed*
with respect to*	*With respect to these difficult choices we are facing*

You are probably familiar with most, if not all, of the topic introducers in Table 8.1 and have probably used some of them in your own writing.

Although you should take care not to overuse topic introducers at the beginning of sentences, these words and phrases along with reference forms are useful sentence connectors. The ones that sound most familiar to you, such as *concerning* or *in regard to*, are most likely those that are most commonly used in different kinds of writing. Others that may sound less familiar, such as *with reference to* and *with respect to,* are used most often in very formal academic writing or formal speech and are less common.

---

* Used primarily in formal contexts, such as a business letter, a legal document, or a speech

---

Exercise 2

Using the phrases in Table 8.1, cross out the incorrectly formed topic introducer in the last sentence of each passage. Then write the correct form in the blank. More than one correct choice is possible.

1. We have received your letter dated October 20, 2014, in which you ask for a full refund. In reference with your letter, we will not be able to fulfill your request without the following documentation. _____

2. There are two possible solutions to this budget problem: negotiate a lower price with our current vendor or find a new vendor willing to come in at a lower price. Regarding to the first option, we will need to send a request to Halsom Equipment by the end of the month. _____

3. Tuition costs are on the rise these days, even for public colleges and universities. As related to this problem is an increase in housing and textbook costs, which makes higher education even less affordable. _____

4. First-generation college students face many challenges at four-year universities, including managing family and work obligations. In regards to family obligations, students feel caught between two worlds—their school and non-school world—often feeling forced to sacrifice their close-knit relationship with their family in order to succeed at the university. _____

Writers often use topic introducers to single out and elaborate on one point from a list of points noted earlier in a passage. This technique is used in this critique of an author's argument about social class and mobility:

> The author presents a number of success stories—compelling descriptions of people born into the lower class who acquire higher education and attain a high socio-economic status. However, I am concerned about his use of evidence and about the conclusions he draws. <u>Regarding the first limitation</u>, I believe that his sources may be biased. The for-profit companies sponsoring this research also sponsor programs in low-income schools, which means that they might gain more support for their programs if the results show success. <u>Concerning the second limitation</u>, I believe the author has over-generalized from too few examples. While individuals may succeed, according to many theorists, on average, people from lower socio-economic backgrounds struggle to achieve the "American Dream."

Exercise 3

Read each passage and consider how the last sentence or sentences relate(s) to the earlier ones. Complete the blank with a reference form and classifier noun. Try to use vocabulary that is new to you.

1. In the past, TV was the favored medium for campaign ads in the U.S. TV ads provide extensive exposure for political candidates, but the costs are high. Running one 30-second ad in primetime can cost between $40,000–$700,000. Now, more and more campaigns use TV airtime sparingly, running ads for a short time before moving the ads to campaign websites for further viewing. Regarding _____, one campaign representative noted, "The Internet has really revolutionized the way we connect with the public, and in a money saving way."

2. The Kyoto Protocol requires developed countries to reduce greenhouse gas emissions and developing countries to monitor and report emissions. As for _____, critics complain that, without involvement from the U.S., a major greenhouse gas emitter, results from the protocol will be limited.

3. Several opponents attempt to show that amnesty programs for immigrants lead to higher unemployment and welfare costs. Amnesty, they worry, can also lead to an increase in terrorism threats and crime. Evidence, however, is inconclusive. In regard to _____, researchers note that immigration may, in fact, have a positive effect on our economy by citing evidence that immigrants do not necessarily take jobs away from U.S. citizens. Regarding _____, many studies show that, by tracking amnestied immigrants, we would have better information on immigrants than we would if they remained illegal.

8.2 USING LOGICAL CONNECTORS WITH REFERENCE FORMS TO CONNECT IDEAS

Building Your Knowledge

Just as topic introducers create explicit connections for the reader across sentences and paragraphs, so do logical connectors. They also help writers condense information into sentences by creating those connections with a phrase, not a longer clause with repetition of wording. Table 8.2 shows an example that illustrates the benefits of using logical connectors with reference forms and noun phrases.

There is nothing grammatically incorrect with the example in the second column, as it clearly connects the recommendation in the third sentence back to the ideas explored in the first two sentences. However, research on academic writing style suggests that the example in the third column is more commonly used. Academic writers tend to use logical connectors with reference forms and noun phrases,

Table 8.2: Cohesion Created through Logical Connectors with Reference Forms

Without a Logical Connector	With a Clause That Creates the Logical Connection through Repetition	With a Logical Connector + Reference Form + Noun Phrase to Echo Ideas
. . . our economic forecasts call for rising pricing pressures and a steady federal funds rate. In short, investors may be disappointed if the Fed doesn't cut rates anytime soon—and we don't think it will. We recently signaled to our investor clients that they should consider paring back the exposure to stocks in their portfolios.	. . . our economic forecasts call for rising pricing pressures and a steady federal funds rate. In short, investors may be disappointed if the Fed doesn't cut rates anytime soon—and we don't think it will. **Because prices will most probably rise and the federal funds rate is probably going to remain steady,** we recently signaled to our investor clients that they should consider paring back the exposure to stocks in their portfolios.	. . . our economic forecasts call for rising pricing pressures and a steady federal funds rate. In short, investors may be disappointed if the Fed doesn't cut rates anytime soon—and we don't think it will. **Given these trends and outlooks,** we recently signaled to our investor clients that they should consider paring back the exposure to stocks in their portfolios.

not clauses with words like *because, since,* or *although,* to create cohesion. This section will provide practice with creating explicit, logical connections with more commonly used academic vocabulary and structures.

Table 8.3 illustrates how to use reference forms with logical connectors to show more complex relationships between ideas.

Table 8.3: Logical Connectors with Reference Forms

Meaning	Logical Connectors	Examples with Reference Forms
assuming or building on ideas	*based on*	*Based on such findings*
	given	*Given such a positive outlook*
	in light of	*In light of these limitations*
	in view of	*In view of this economic fact*
showing the result or effect of previous ideas	*because of*	*Because of this imbalance*
	due to	*Due to this disparity*
	on account of	*On account of the pollution*
	as a result of	*As a result of these efforts*
introducing a result not influenced by a previous factor	*despite*	*Despite such safeguards*
	regardless of	*Regardless of these limitations*
showing similar traits	*like* *similar to*	*Like this previous example* *Similar to these approaches*
setting up a contrast to highlight difference	*contrary to*	*Contrary to this belief*
	in contrast to	*In contrast to such a position*
	*compared to**	*Compared to such drastic changes*
	*in comparison to**	*In comparison to the body of research on X*
	*comparing X and/with Y**	*Comparing these results with those of a previous study*
	different from	*Different from previous models*
	unlike	*Unlike these larger groups*
adding another point	*in addition to*	*In addition to these strategies*
	along with	*Along with this economic trend*

* Despite the use of the words *compared* and *comparison*, these connectors usually highlight difference.

Exercise 4

Read the paragraphs and think about how the last sentence or sentences relate(s) to the earlier ones. Complete the blank with a logical connector + reference form + classifier noun. Try to use vocabulary that is new to you. The first one has been done for you as an example.

1. Tomorrow night, we are organizing the charity dinner for our client's organization. According to my notes, the chef has planned an Italian menu. I have just learned that one colleague is allergic to wheat; one is vegetarian; and one likes to avoid acidic food. <u>In light of these dietary restrictions</u>, we need to meet with the chef to change the menu plan.

2. Over the past several years, the public has received more and more negative information about eating fast food. The nutritional value of fast food has been questioned: often fast food lacks vegetables and whole grains, which provide nutrients and fiber. This food may contain large quantities of sugar, fat, and salt, which have been linked to obesity and Type II diabetes. _____, more and more people seem to be eating at fast food restaurants, probably for the convenience and low prices.

3. The fast food industry, however, has responded. Now customers are greeted with signs on the windows of restaurants stating that the food is made without transfats. And menus have begun to include salads, fruit, and lighter options that are lower in fat and carbohydrates. In fact, restaurants even publish the nutritional information about each item on the menu. _____, it might now be possible to find healthier options at fast food restaurants.

4. In recent years, more and more people in the U.S. have begun to purchase organic food. People tend to buy organic because they want to avoid pesticides and artificial additives, which can be dangerous to our health. Also, people prefer organic production because it uses fewer toxins and thus spares the environment. _____, people choose organic food because it is associated with better working conditions for the farmers who work in the fields.

5. Starting in the mid-1990s, as the popularity of organic food began to increase in the U.S., organic food production has experienced annual increases that far surpass growth in the rest of the food industry. No longer is organic food available only at local farmers' markets; large, complex national networks of production and distribution have been created. _____, the price of organic foods has dropped dramatically.

Using Logical Connectors to Express Differences

A number of logical connectors in English can indicate contrast, such as *however, on the other hand,* and *conversely.* The connectors emphasized in this chapter differ from these connectors because instead of introducing a new sentence, they combine with noun phrases.

However

Some people believe X. *However,* **others believe** Y.

In contrast to

In contrast to **this belief**, others believe Y.

The forms shown in Table 8.4 are sometimes challenging to use correctly. *Contrary to* and *in contrast to* do not have the same meanings. As for the connector *compared to,* the past participle form *compared* is sometimes confused with the present participle form *comparing.* Review the forms and meanings, including ungrammatical forms that should be avoided. (NP=noun phrase.)

Table 8.4: Contrast and Comparison Connectors with Reference Forms

Cohesive Forms	Examples	Meanings and Usage Notes
contrary to [NP]	Many people think that bats are blind. *Contrary to this widely held belief,* healthy bats are not blind, but they depend highly on their sense of smell rather than sight during the night.	*Contrary to* expresses an idea that disagrees with the previous statement (e.g., bats are blind), suggesting that the previous statement is not true (e.g., Bats are not blind–they just don't use their eyesight much). This connector is often used to introduce information that contradicts a commonly held belief or opinion.
in contrast to [NP]	Most animals are diurnal; that is, they are active during the day and sleep at night. *In contrast to this group,* nocturnal animals, such as bats, are active at night.	*In contrast to* expresses a difference from something previously mentioned. Unlike *contrary to*, it does not mean that the earlier idea is untrue.
in comparison to [NP] **compared to [NP]**	According to one national survey, college students today are more focused on financial success than they were a few decades ago. *In comparison to / compared to* that earlier period, students today have greater expectations that college will prepare them for a well-paying job.	*In comparison to* and *compared to* can both be used to contrast an idea in a previous sentence with a new idea.
comparing [NP] **with/to/and [NP]**	*Comparing this most recent survey with previous ones,* it is clear that students today find college more stressful than they did in the past. *Comparing the earlier and subsequent results,* we see little difference between the two. *Comparing this concert to street noise* is insulting!	With two noun phrases, *comparing* requires the preposition *with* or *to* or the conjunction *and* between the phrases. In academic English, use *with* when like things are compared (e.g., two surveys). Use *to* for comparison of unlike things (e.g., a concert and street noise). Note that unlike *compared*, *comparing* is followed by a noun phrase. We do not use *to* directly after this form. NOT: *Comparing to* the earlier results…
comparing [NP plural]	*Comparing the five reviews* of this film, we can see that there was much disagreement about its merits.	*Comparing* can also be followed by a plural noun phrase.

Exercise 5

Circle the connector that you think best links the sentences.

1. Bats are the only mammals that can fly. As a result, they are often described as having wings. *Contrary to / In contrast to* this common misconception, bats do not have wings but rather modified hands; their elongated fingers support membranes that allow sustained flight.

2. Both sea otters and harbor seals are marine mammals that live in kelp forest habitats and go onto land to breed and produce young. They differ, however, in physical characteristics. *Contrary to / in contrast to* sea otters, harbor seals have flippers instead of paws and no visible earflaps.

3. It is commonly believed in western cultures that expressing anger is healthy. In a recently published book, a clinical psychologist argues that, *contrary to / in contrast to* this popular wisdom, expressing anger directly will often make a bad situation worse.

4. The Civil War general Abner Doubleday is thought to have invented baseball in 1839 in Cooperstown, New York. *Contrary to / In contrast to* this continuing myth, historians have identified references to baseball going back to the 1820s, and in fact there may have been no single inventor of the game.

5. Saturated fats found in meat and dairy products are known to create health risks for humans when consumed in large amounts over long periods of time. *Contrary to / In contrast to* these so-called bad fats are essential fatty acids, which raise good cholesterol and can repair damage done by the bad fats.

Exercise 6

Identify and cross out the incorrectly formed comparison connector in the last sentence of each passage. Then write the correct form in the blank. More than one correct form is possible.

1. According to *Ethnologue*, a reference cataloging all the known living languages, there are 6,912 living languages in the world today. If we look at the numbers of languages within continents, there are striking differences. Africa and Europe are good examples. Compare to Europe, which currently has 230 living languages, or 3.5% of total languages of the world, Africa has 2,092, representing almost a third of all living languages.

   _____

2. Although Africa is second only to Asia in its number of living languages, many of the individual languages are not used by many speakers. Again in comparison Europe, African languages account for only 11.8% of speakers of the world, while European languages account for 26.3% of all speakers.

   _____

3. One of the challenges of learning a second language is mastering the vowel system of that language. Languages of the world differ considerably in the number of vowel sounds they have. English is considered to have an uncommonly large number of vowels. For example, comparing to Spanish, English has six more vowels.

   _____

4. Cultures differ in their views of politeness in different situations such as making requests, complaining, or giving and accepting compliments. One recent article reviewed how people from five different cultures differed in expressing compliments. Compare Egyptians with Americans, the study noted that Egyptians do not offer compliments as frequently as Americans and that they often express compliments regarding natural appearances and personal traits.

   _____

Part 3: Qualifying Ideas and Reporting Research

Chapter 9: Expressing Degrees of Certainty and Accuracy

In academic writing, writers often need to qualify statements with vocabulary that expresses degrees of certainty or accuracy about the information they are conveying. These words and phrases are known as **hedges**. For example, instead of stating that a result will definitely follow from an action, a writer may say that it *could* happen or that it will happen *in some situations*. In English, writers can choose from many types of hedging words and expressions that serve different purposes.

Raising Language Awareness

Exercise 1

Discuss the differences between the first and second sentences in each pair. Focus on the use of hedges and the impact on the information expressed.

1. a. Increased communication between parents and children helps parents gauge their child's emotional state.

   b. Increased communication between parents and children may help parents gauge their child's emotional state.

2. a. As more studies are completed, other drug interactions will be detected.

   b. As more studies are completed, it is likely that other drug interactions will be detected.

3. a. Reducing intake of animal fat will lead to better health.

   b. Reducing intake of animal fat will potentially lead to better health.

4. a. According to research, strong and effective readers preview texts and make predictions about content before reading.

   b. According to research, strong and effective readers tend to preview texts and make predictions about content before reading.

5. a. Symptoms of Alzheimer's disease appear after age 60.

   b. Symptoms of Alzheimer's disease typically appear after age 60.

Exercise 2

Identify the words and phrases used to qualify statements in each passage. The first one in Item 1 has been done for you as an example. The number of qualifying words/phrases is given in parentheses.

1. What techniques are effective for individual learning? Recent research reveals that the advice offered in <u>generally</u> study skills courses is in fact wrong. For example, these courses typically encourage students to find a specific, quiet place to study; however, psychologists have found that students may learn more if their study contexts are varied. It is possible that this improved learning occurs because the brain is able to make multiple associations with the same materials, which slows down forgetting. Another study habit that seems to improve learning is varying the kinds of material studied at one time, such as vocabulary and speaking in language learning. It appears that mixing the types of materials learned leaves a deeper impression on the brain. One piece of advice that does hold true is cramming, as cramming does not, in most cases, lead to retention of information over time. While cramming might improve one's test score on a particular exam, information learned will probably be forgotten soon afterward. (9)

2. During the last decade, school systems have tended to decrease their focus on the fine arts in order to stress core subjects such as reading and mathematics. However, a growing body of research suggests that instruction in the arts could improve student learning across all disciplines. A four-year study at Boston College indicates that students who get musical training experience structural changes in the brain. Despite these intriguing findings, conclusions of current research sometimes do not translate directly to classrooms. The next probable area of focus, according to University of Oregon researcher Michael Posner, will explore the connection that most scientists believe most likely exists between the study of music and math ability. (5)

3. With economic changes in work environments nationwide, American workers today frequently complain about workload. Employees often feel pressured to work extra hours and/or to give up vacation or sick days to get work done. Professional workers routinely extend their work time into the weekends and holidays. In one study, parents stated they hardly ever had time to spend with their children due to work hours. With continued downsizing and mergers occurring in workplaces, the problems of work overload for employees are unlikely to improve in the near future. (5)

Building Your Knowledge

Using Modal Verbs

When academic writers discuss complex topics, it is often difficult to be completely certain that something will happen or that one cause will always lead to a specific effect. Because writers cannot always be sure that their observations or results are completely accurate, they use hedges to make their points.

Here is an example from Exercise 1:

Increased communication between parents and children helps parents gauge their child's emotional state.

Increased communication between parents and children <u>may</u> help parents gauge their child's emotional state.

In the second sentence, the writer chooses to use the word *may* to express uncertainty. Of course, parents hope that increased communication will always lead to a clearer understanding of how their children are doing, but interactions between parents and children are complex. Parents may hear what they want to hear or jump to conclusions about what their children are saying or thinking. Children may not share or may even try to cover up their true thoughts. And if one side gets mad at the other, the groups may not listen well to each other.

Notice in the explanation that we used the word *may* several times to show that there is a possibility, perhaps a small one, that the communication will not lead to better understanding. Academic writers try to account for this possibility by using hedging devices. The most common hedging device is the use of a modal verb: *can, could, may, might,* or *should.*

Some more examples showing a possibility but not certainty are:

The consumption of fish oil <u>might</u> reduce hypertension.

The warm "Loop Current" in the Gulf of Mexico <u>may</u> account for the large number of hurricanes.

The high incidence of violence <u>can</u> be attributed to poverty levels.

Interest rates <u>could</u> remain stable throughout the year.

If proper survey procedures are followed, we <u>should</u> gain valid information about consumer perceptions.

Writers may also hedge with *can, could, may,* or *might* when they want to make a recommendation without sounding too forceful or take a position, especially one that may counter previous beliefs. Academic writers enter into conversations with other writers. While they may assert their own opinions, they want to be careful, polite, and diplomatic. Hedging devices provide a good strategy for achieving these goals.

An example of making a recommendation is:

Further research <u>may</u> be needed to confirm Henderson's results.
(We don't want to make Henderson and his study look bad!)

An example of giving a position is:

One lesson we <u>might</u> take from this study is that previous theories <u>may</u> be too simplistic.
(We don't want to suggest that we are smarter than all the previous scholars!)

Exercise 3

Read this summary of an article on happiness. Then complete the sentences using information from the summary. More than one answer is possible.

> Even though prosperity and quality of life have increased, Americans' overall happiness has not increased, according to recent polls. Studies show that happiness is based in part on genetics but there are also ways people can increase their happiness. They can achieve greater happiness not through amassing money or taking anti-depressants, but through feeling grateful, optimistic, and forgiving; forming strong friendships; and creating "flow"—a feeling developed via creative and playful activity.

1. [Possibility] The happiness that athletes, musicians, writers, gamers, and religious adherents feel could be due to _____

   _____ .

2. [Possibility] _____

   _____

   might lead to increased happiness.

3. [Recommendation] In order to increase one's level of happiness, a person might want to _____

   _____ .

4. [Recommendation] Given recent research results, in order to increase employee morale, employers should _____

   _____ .

Using Adjectives of Probability

In addition to using modals, writers can use adjectives of probability to qualify predictions and explore alternative views on a particular topic.

Table 9.1 highlights some common adjectives of probability and the grammatical environments in which they most frequently appear.

Table 9.1: Adjectives of Probability

Probability Adjective + Grammatical Environment	Sample Sentences
It is *likely* that *probable* *possible* *unlikely* *doubtful*	• *It is doubtful that* Congress will approve the bill.
Determiner + *likely* + noun *probable* *possible* *unlikely* *doubtful*	• *One likely outcome* is that Congress will fail to reach a compromise. • *A possible solution* could be a compromise between the two parties. • *Some probable consequences* include late-night negotiations and a last-minute compromise.
to be + *likely* *probable* *possible* *unlikely* *doubtful*	• A positive outcome *is doubtful*.
to be + *likely* + *to* verb *unlikely*	• Congress *is unlikely to reach* a compromise by the deadline. • In the past, progress *was likely to occur* when both sides were willing to compromise.

Exercise 4

Replace the underlined hedge with the hedge listed in parentheses. Make other changes to the verb as needed. The first one has been done for you as an example.

1. Saturn's moon Titan <u>might have</u> liquid mixtures below its surface. (*it is likely that*)

   It is likely that Saturn's moon has liquid mixtures below its

   surface.

2. Next year's basketball season <u>may not start</u> on time because the players are on strike. (noun + *to be unlikely to*) _____

   _____ .

3. The gas and dust surrounding black holes <u>could be</u> the source of high-energy cosmic rays. (*one possible* + noun) _____

   _____ .

4. Given recent research results, the state of Michigan <u>may now use</u> this new method to increase iodine in table salt. (*it is probable that*)

   _____

   _____ .

5. Microsoft <u>may not be able to reverse</u> this downward trend. (noun + *to be doubtful*) _____

   _____ .

6. According to scientists, sudden acceleration <u>could be caused</u> by internal electromagnetic interference, not floor mats and sticky gas pedals. (*a likely* + noun)

   _____

   _____ .

Modifying Probability Adjectives with *Highly*

Many writers modify the probability adjectives to increase the intensity of the claim but still show a lack of certainty. Some examples with *highly* are shown. <u>Note</u>: *Highly* is not commonly used with the adjective *possible*.

> It is <u>highly doubtful</u> that Congress will approve the bill.

> One <u>highly likely</u> outcome is that Congress will fail to reach a compromise.

> Some <u>highly probable</u> consequences include late-night negotiations and a last-minute compromise.

> A positive outcome is <u>highly doubtful</u>.

> Congress is <u>highly unlikely</u> to reach a compromise by the deadline.

> In the past, progress was <u>highly likely</u> to occur when both sides were willing to compromise.

Exercise 5

Table 9.2 lists 12 factors employees note are important to their job satisfaction and the percentage of employees satisfied with each factor. Imagine that you are working in the human resources division of a company in which job morale seems low. Write sentences about the current situation in the company and make projections about the future using the information in Table 9.2 and the expressions given in the parentheses. The first one has been done for you as an example.

Table 9.2: Important Aspects of Job Satisfaction Based on Employee Surveys

Opportunities to use skills/abilities	63%
Job security	61%
Compensation / Pay	60%
Communication between employees and senior management	57%
Relationship with immediate supervisor	54%
Benefits (health insurance, retirement, etc.)	53%
Organization's financial stability	52%
The work itself	52%
Management's recognition of employee job performance	50%
Autonomy and independence	48%
Flexibility to balance life and work issues	46%
Career advancement opportunities	42%

Adapted from Society for Human Resource Management (2012). *2012 Employee Job Satisfaction and Engagement: How Employees Are Dealing With Uncertainty.* Arlington, VA: SHRM. Retrieved from http://www.shrm.org/research/surveyfindings/articles/pages/2012employeejobsatisfaction.aspx

1. (*The most probable explanation for*) ____The most probable____ explanation for low morale is employees' belief that their skills are underutilized.

2. (*Another probable cause of*) _____

_____

_____.

3. (*is highly likely to*) _____

_____

_____.

4. (*It is unlikely that*) _____

_____

_____.

5. (Noun + *is highly doubtful*) _____

_____

_____.

6. (*Some possible solutions*) _____

_____

_____.

Using Adverbs of Probability

Just as writers can use adjectives to show probability, they can also use adverbs. Some common probability adverbs are *likely, perhaps, possibly, potentially*, and *probably*. Example sentences using a probability adverb are shown.

1. We recommend investing in sturdy garbage bins with tight-fitting lids to keep neighborhood cats from eating <u>potentially</u> dangerous leftovers like chicken bones or spoiled meat.

2. Several neighborhood cats have recently become ill. We think that these cats <u>probably</u> ate something dangerous in people's garbage.

3. Stray cats will <u>likely</u> try to gain access to leftover food in people's trash. Neighbors are encouraged to purchase sturdy garbage bins with tight-fitting lids.

4. Several neighborhood cats have recently become ill. <u>Perhaps</u> they have gotten into the trash and eaten something dangerous.

5. The increasing number of cats getting into neighborhood trash is <u>possibly</u> due to flimsy garbage cans.

6. An increasingly large number of cats have gotten into neighborhood trash, <u>possibly</u> due to flimsy garbage cans without tight-fitting lids.

7. Many cats have taken ill. Leftover food that cats can easily access has <u>most probably</u> created this problem.

8. Many cats can get into people's trash and eat leftover food, <u>possibly</u> resulting in illness or even death.

Exercise 6

Analyze the eight example sentences on page 186 and discuss answers to these questions with a partner or in a small group.

1. In Sentence 1, what word is *potentially* describing? What part of speech is that word?

   _____

   _____

2. In Sentences 2 and 3, the probability adverb is describing a verb. Where exactly should a writer put a probability adverb in relation to the verb?

   _____

   _____

3. What is different about the placement of *perhaps* in Sentence 4?

   _____

   _____

4. Look at the COCA academic register results in the chart. Which placement is more common in academic writing—close to the verb or at the beginning of the sentence?

   _____

   _____

	Beginning of Sentence	**Close to Verb**
likely	23	2518
perhaps	4225	1011
possibly	154	963
potentially	42	850
probably	261	3669

5. Sentences 5–8 illustrate different ways writers use probability adverbs to show cause and effect. In Sentence 5, why is the placement of the probability adverb different from its placement in Sentences 2, 3, and 7?

   _____

   _____

Exercise 7

Review Table 9.2 again. Create sentences about job dissatisfaction at a company you work for or want to work for using the probability adverb in parentheses. The first one has been done for you as an example.

What are some possible causes of job dissatisfaction?

1. (*is possibly due to*)   The current drop in employee morale is

possibly due to worries about decreased benefits.

2. (*, possibly due to*) _____

_____.

3. (*likely stem(s) from*) _____

_____.

4. (*perhaps*) _____

_____.

What recommendations can you provide?

5. (*potentially useful*) _____

_____.

6. (*will possibly lead to*) _____

_____.

Using Verbs of Uncertainty

Another common hedging device is the use of the verbs *seem, appear,* and *tend* to make claims a little softer or sound more polite.

Table 9.3 highlights the most common uses of these hedges.

Table 9.3: Hedging Verbs

Grammatical Structure	Common Collocations	Sample Sentences
appear + to + verb	*be* (common) *be + -ing* verb *confirm* *correspond* *correlate with* *contradict*	This type of health care *appears to be* the most cost-effective. Health care costs *appear to be growing* faster than workers can afford. The results *appear to confirm* our initial claim.
It appears that	none	*It appears that* male participants favored working alone.
seems to + verb	*be* *have* *suggest* *indicate* *agree with* *fit* *confirm* *correspond* *contradict*	Unfortunately, plagiarism *seems to be* a growing trend at U.S. universities. The military is the only institution that *seems to have* the capacity to oversee elections. Our results *seem to suggest* that racial divisions still exist.
seems/appears to + have + verb	*have been* *have become* *have changed*	Temperature *seems to have been* a factor. Investing in real estate *appears to have become* riskier in recent years.
It seems that	none	*It seems that* families with two working parents spend less time cooking and more money eating out.
seems + adjective	*clear* *reasonable* *appropriate* *logical* *odd* *surprising*	Further investigation into this problem *seems appropriate*. It *seems clear* that implementing the new safety precautions has been beneficial. It *seems reasonable* to expect continued resistance from the rebel group.
tend + to + verb	*be* *focus on* *view* *agree* *favor* *increase* *produce*	Politicians *tend to agree* on tax breaks during election years. During mid- to late summer, the frogs' period of inactivity *tends to be* longer.

Exercise 8

Each sentence is based on a study of boys and girls in co-educational and single-sex schools and their involvement in sports. Using information from Table 9.3, add the hedging verb in parentheses after each sentence to soften the claim. Make other changes in structure and wording as necessary. More than one answer is possible for some items. The first one has been done for you as an example.

1. Our previous thinking about gender and competition in sports is incorrect. (appear)

   It appears that our previous thinking… OR Our previous thinking about … appears to be incorrect.

2. According to the results of this new study, adolescent girls enrolled in co-educational schools during their adolescent years shied away from competition. (tend)

3. However, the girls from single-sex schools entered competitions as often as boys. (seem)

4. A girl's school environment plays an important role in her choice to compete. (appear)

5. These results contradict earlier beliefs about gender and involvement in sports. (appear)

6. Such behavior is learned, not genetic. (seem)

Using Frequency Adverbs

When writers want to avoid generalizations, they often use frequency adverbs. These adverbs can express a wide range of frequencies between the absolutes of *always* and *never*. They are especially helpful when writers want to express the idea of things that typically or usually occur or hold true but wish to avoid claiming that something happens or is the case 100 percent of the time. Some common frequency adverbs are listed in Table 9.4.

Table 9.4: Frequency Adverbs

almost always	in most cases	ordinarily	typically
almost never	normally	rarely	usually
at times	often	routinely	
generally	on average	seldom	
hardly ever	on occasion	sometimes	

Exercise 9

Sort the frequency words and phrases in Table 9.4 depending on whether they indicate high frequency or low frequency.

High Frequency	Low Frequency
almost always	almost never

Expressing Normal or Usual Patterns

The adverbs *generally*, *in most cases*, *normally*, *on average*, *ordinarily*, *typically*, and *usually* all describe events or situations that hold true much of the time or happen during normal processes. However, some of these adverbs tend to be used more frequently than others, and one of them, *ordinarily*, is sometimes used in a context when an exception is being noted.

Exercise 10

Check the frequencies of these adverbs in COCA and complete the chart. The first one has been done for you as an example. Note that it is based on 2015 data; you may want to check to see if it has changed.

Adverb	Frequencies in COCA
generally	16,819
in most cases	
normally	
often	
on average	
ordinarily	
routinely	
typically	
usually	

Exercise 11

Circle the hedging adverbs in each example taken or adapted from COCA. The first one has been done for you as an example.

1. Solar radiation would (normally) reach the earth within a few days.

2. Often the large African masks in our collection deliberately include ferocious animal features to frighten onlookers.

3. It typically takes eight to ten years to build a nuclear power plant.

4. Many music teachers routinely rely on curriculum models that are academic and that emphasize facts over music.

5. In most cases, the content of a physical education curriculum consists of more than team sports.

6. In public hospitals, people whose social worlds do not ordinarily intersect share intimate space and daily routines.

7. The survey took 37.5 minutes on average to complete.

8. At a variety of interactive displays, you can experience colors as other animals do, including parts of the spectrum that are normally imperceptible to humans.

9. In Singapore, athletes usually believe that coaches employed by schools are experts in their fields.

10. Throughout much of his career, Robert Mitchum was generally regarded less as an actor than as a personality.

Now summarize the rule for placement of the frequency adverb when it modifies an auxiliary (*be, have,* modal such as *would*) + verb.

The frequency adverb is placed _____.

Exercise 12

Choose the hedging adverb or adverb phrase that best fits the context of the sentence and then rewrite that portion of the sentence. Use the information in parentheses to guide your choice. The first one has been done for you as an example. More than one position is possible.

1. College students complete their degrees in four years. (Many do, but there are also many exceptions.)

   (a.) generally   b. in most cases   c. normally

   College students generally complete

2. Safety checks are made on automobiles before they leave the factory. (Mechanics do this as a part of the normal process; exceptions might occur but would not be acceptable.)

   a. generally   b. often   c. routinely

   _____

3. You can't see the sun's corona from the earth. (An exception is during a solar eclipse.)

   a. often   b. ordinarily   c. on average

   _____

4. The Mainland Airlines flights have arrived on time this year. (They arrived on time only 10 out of 100 times.)

   a. typically   b. normally   c. seldom

   _____

5. The company's Chief Executive Officer projects 20% annual profits for the next five years. (The profits may not be exactly the same each year.)

   a. typically   b. on average   c. routinely

   _____

Adding Hedges

Some students are nervous about using hedges because they are worried that their claims will not sound strong enough. However, students who do not use hedges risk making claims that they cannot support. Unfortunately, the claims are usually too strong and can easily be challenged.

Exercise 13

Add at least one hedging device where necessary to make these claims more defensible. Try to use different ones in each sentence to practice using a variety of hedges and/or use more than one if necessary. The first one has been done for you as an example.

1. Future studies ~~will~~ *could* benefit from finer distinctions among different aspects of employee performance.

2. Increasing discussion about racism in the community will create more unity and reduce anger.

3. Western doctors are never educated in herbal treatments and thus always think that chemical treatments are better than natural ones.

4. Non-native speakers always struggle with the pronunciation of the English *r*-sound.

5. Housing prices in all neighborhoods across the country are still declining.

6. Poverty is caused by a lack of education.

Chapter 10: Using Reporting Verbs

Academic writing is sometimes thought of as a "conversation" between a writer and others who have discussed the same topic or engaged in similar research. Chapter 9 looked at how writers use hedging devices to qualify statements in order to best represent their positions in that conversation. Much academic writing also involves using source materials written by others. Writers use sources to provide a context for their own ideas and to compare or contrast their ideas with others. In some cases, a writer may be reviewing or evaluating what someone else has written; that is, the focus of the piece of writing may be a summary and response to a single text.

In academic writing, we use many verbs when referring to sources. Such verbs are often called **reporting verbs** because we use them to cite another's ideas and to attribute those ideas to the author or source, whether as a quote, a paraphrase, or a summary. More general reporting verbs—like *ask*, *say*, or *write*—can be used in many environments. However, many reporting verbs used in academic prose carry very specific meanings. Therefore, writers must be careful to use reporting verbs appropriately depending on the author's meanings and the rhetorical contexts of their own writing. Using an appropriate verb involves much more than just knowledge of a dictionary definition. This chapter will help you make good choices. In this chapter, *writer* refers to the person who is using the sources; *author* refers to the source being cited.

Raising Language Awareness

Exercise 1

Circle the verbs used to report on a source in each passage. The number of reporting verbs in each passage is given in parentheses. The first one has been done for you as an example.

1. A recent study in the journal *Science* (indicates) that Tibetans have developed a unique form of a gene allowing them to thrive at altitudes above 14,000 feet. The research group, led by a UC Berkeley biologist, found that the DNA of Tibetans differed from the Han Chinese with whom they are closely related ethnically. The genetic variant was identified in 87% of Tibetans and only 9% of Han Chinese. Researchers determined that these two ethnic groups separated from each other about 3,000 years ago. As John Hawks, an anthropologist at the University of Wisconsin, pointed out, in evolutionary terms, this is not the distant past. The rapid evolutionary change was explained by the need for Tibetans to adapt quickly in the harsh environment of the Himalayas. (6)

2. In *The Facebook Effect*, David Kirkpatrick, a *Fortune* magazine reporter, presents the first authoritative account of the founding of Facebook, the social media network. The early days of the company's formation are described in detail, including many humorous anecdotes about the founder, Harvard student Mark Zuckerberg. Kirkpatrick reveals that Zuckerberg from the start wanted to change the world with Facebook, to make it "a more open place." Kirkpatrick provides little information about some of the current problems with Facebook users' personal data; on the other hand, he does not dismiss concerns that Facebook may become less a place for friendship and more of a place for marketing. (5)

3. Reporting on recent studies on the effects of birth order on personality, Harvard researcher Joshua K. Hartshorne acknowledges that most previous studies have not supported links between birth order and personality or behavior. He notes, for example, that cognitive scientist Steven Pinker has rejected the notion that birth order is relevant in the discussion of nature vs. nurture in cognitive development. Hartshorne counters these findings with those of recent research. He offers evidence from his own research that suggests birth order influences whom people select for friends and spouses. (7)

You have probably come across many reporting verbs in your academic reading and have likely used a number of them in your own writing. Table 10.1 lists some of the most common reporting verbs.

Exercise 2

Put a **+** in the blank next to the reporting verbs that you use in your own writing. Put a **√** next to those that you know but rarely use. Put a **−** next to words you are not familiar with and do not use.

Table 10.1: Reporting Verbs

__acknowledge	__consider	__examine	__note	__reject
__advise	__contend	__explain	__object to	__remark
__advocate	__contrast	__fail	__observe	__report
__analyze	__counter	__favor	__offer	__reveal
__argue	__criticize	__find	__oppose	__show
__assert	__demand	__focus on	__point out	__speculate
__assume	__demonstrate	__give	__predict	__state
__believe	__deny	__identify	__present	__stress
__call for	__describe	__imply	__propose	__study
__caution	__determine	__indicate	__prove	__suggest
__challenge	__develop	__insist	__provide	__summarize
__claim	__discuss	__investigate	__question	__support
__comment	__dismiss	__list	__realize	__think
__compare	__dispute	__maintain	__recognize	__urge
__conclude	__distinguish	__mention	__recommend	__warn
__confirm	__emphasize	__neglect	__refute	__wonder

Exercise 3

Circle the reporting verb and underline the grammatical structure following each verb. Then write C in the blank if the underlined structure is correct and can be used after that reporting verb. Write I if the structure is incorrect and cannot be used after that verb. The first one has been done for you as an example.

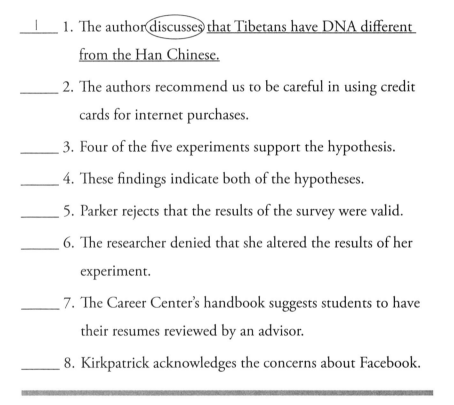

   __I__   1. The author (discusses) that Tibetans have DNA different from the Han Chinese.

   _____   2. The authors recommend us to be careful in using credit cards for internet purchases.

   _____   3. Four of the five experiments support the hypothesis.

   _____   4. These findings indicate both of the hypotheses.

   _____   5. Parker rejects that the results of the survey were valid.

   _____   6. The researcher denied that she altered the results of her experiment.

   _____   7. The Career Center's handbook suggests students to have their resumes reviewed by an advisor.

   _____   8. Kirkpatrick acknowledges the concerns about Facebook.

Building Your Knowledge

Reporting on an Author's Strength of Claim and Emphasis

The selection of a reporting verb will be based on your interpretation of the author's stance; that is, you may want your readers to know whether an author feels strongly or confident about a claim or, in contrast, whether the author wants to be more tentative about that claim.

What do you see as the difference in the author's stance depending on the choice of reporting verb for this statement?

The author
$\left.\begin{array}{l} \text{argues} \\ \text{suggests} \end{array}\right\}$ that high school arts programs deserve more support.

As this example shows, reporting verbs can help to convey strongly felt opinions as well as ideas that represent only suggestions or proposals.

Verbs that express the strength of a claim are used not only when the subject is a person but also when the subject is an abstract noun, such as a belief, a finding, or a result. Again, consider the difference in strength of claim conveyed by these reporting verbs.

The preliminary results
$\left.\begin{array}{l} \text{confirm} \\ \text{indicate} \end{array}\right\}$ that dust blown off dry fields contains PM-10.

Like the verb *suggest*, the verb *indicate* expresses a weaker belief that the information is true. Especially in reporting research, authors usually use strong verbs only when they are sure of their results.

In addition to expressing the strength of a claim, reporting verbs can convey your interpretation of the importance of the information you are summarizing from an essay or research study. As an example, consider the differences in these two verbs:

The author
$\left.\begin{array}{l} \text{stresses} \\ \text{notes} \end{array}\right\}$ that this approach has limited use.

While the verb *stresses* indicates that the author emphasized the point that follows, the verb *notes* may be used for something that is worth mentioning but is not necessarily so important. This verb choice does not mean that the information is unimportant, but it is likely less important than other points.

Exercise 4

Answer the questions about reporting verb meanings by circling your choices. Then compare your answers with a partner or in a small group.

1. Which three verbs could introduce an author's strong claim?

   assert   claim   contend   note   remark

2. Which three verbs could introduce a weak or tentative claim?

   confirm   maintain   propose   speculate   suggest

3. Which three verbs could introduce a paraphrase or quotation that represents an important point the author wishes to make?

   emphasize   focus on   mention   say   stress

4. Which three verbs could introduce a paraphrase or quotation that represents a point of lesser importance?

   assert   mention   note   remark   urge

5. Which three verbs could introduce a paraphrase or quotation in which the author offers advice to readers?

   caution   deny   indicate   warn   urge

Exercise 5

Imagine that you want to reference information in each passage for a writing assignment. Choose the summary sentence that you think most accurately summarizes the information, the author's stance, and/or strength of claim. Circle the letter of your choice and be prepared to explain. The first one has been done for you as an example.

1. According to Patricia Greenfield, UCLA distinguished professor of psychology, increased exposure to technology has improved our visual skills. Based on analysis of more than 50 studies of learning and technology, Greenfield said that what is known as visual intelligence has been rising globally for the last 50 years.

   a. Professor Patricia Greenfield predicts that our visual skills will get better.

   b. Research on learning and technology, according to Professor Patricia Greenfield, indicates that our visual intelligence has improved worldwide during the past five decades.

   c. Professor Patricia Greenfield explains why technology has increased visual skills.

   Explanation: In a., *predicts* is not appropriate because Greenfield is talking about the present not some future event. In c., *explains* is not accurate because there is no explanation in this passage. The verb *indicates* in b. appropriately expresses the idea that the studies analyzed have shown an increase in visual intelligence.

2. Greenfield believes that increased use of technology is responsible for much of the change in visual skills. However, she thinks that, in addition to this reason, other factors may have contributed to the change. As some examples, she cites a rise in the levels of education, better nutrition around the world, and increased complexity of societies.

   a. Greenfield identifies several other factors besides use of technology that she feels may have influenced the global rise in visual skills.

   b. Greenfield confirms that several other factors have caused a rise in visual intelligence.

   c. Greenfield argues that many factors other than technology are responsible for changes in visual skills.

   Explanation: _____

   _____

   _____

   _____

3. The studies that Greenfield analyzed also show students today are reading less for pleasure. Greenfield says that this kind of reading enhances our thinking abilities and develops imagination in ways that visual media like video games do not. Greenberg says that "most visual media are real-time media that do not allow time for reflection, analysis or imagination."

   a. Greenfield deplores the lack of reading for pleasure.

   b. Greenfield compares the benefits of reading for pleasure to that of using visual media.

   c. Greenfield favors reading for pleasure over video game playing.

   Explanation: _____

   _____

   _____

   _____

4. Studies also looked at the effects of multi-tasking in lecture classes. Students who had access to the internet during classroom lectures did not perform as well on tests after lectures as students who did not have internet access. Interpreting these studies, Greenfield says, "Wiring classrooms for internet access does not enhance learning."

   Based on studies examining students multi-tasking in the classroom,

   a. Greenfield disputes that multi-tasking occurs with access to the internet.

   b. Greenfield warns that we should never wire classrooms for internet access.

   c. Greenfield concludes that classroom learning is not necessarily improved by access to the internet.

   Explanation: _____

   _____

   _____

   _____

5. On the other hand, some jobs demand skill in multi-tasking. Greenfield says that pilots, for example, often have to be paying attention to multiple instruments. Similarly, cab drivers need to be aware of multiple events simultaneously. Many military positions also demand the ability to multi-task.

   a. Greenfield counters the claim that professions demand skill in multi-tasking.

   b. Greenfield supports multi-tasking for some jobs.

   c. Greenfield offers examples of jobs that require multi-tasking abilities.

   Explanation: _____

   _____

   _____

   _____

Using Reporting Verbs with Inanimate Subjects

Some verbs such as *confirm* and *indicate* can be used not only with people as the subject but also with inanimate subjects. An inanimate subject could be an abstract noun (e.g., *beliefs, findings*), a kind of text (e.g., *article*), or a part of a text (e.g., *figure*).

Exercise 6

Circle the inanimate subject and underline the reporting verb(s) in these sentences from the Michigan Corpus of Upper-level Student Papers (MICUSP). The first one has been done for you as an example.

1. (This report) studies the correlation between the percentage changes in Singapore's Straits Times Industrial Index (STI) with the percentage changes in other key financial stock indexes... from the period of January 2004 to August 2007.

2. The following figures investigate these changes further.

3. This paper first discusses some case studies of tall buildings which have advantageously incorporated outrigger beams in their design, and then explores some of the solutions which have been proposed in the literature... .

4. Figure 3 shows 1990 and 2000 census data for college degrees from regular institutions of higher learning (bachelor's and graduate degrees) by age in 1990.

5. Table C examines the relationship between alcoholism, a behavioral variable, and suicide.

6. The results of this investigation reveal that adults did indeed play a necessary role in the formation and development of Nicaraguan Sign Language.

Learning the Grammar of Reporting Verbs

Knowing how to use reporting verbs appropriately also means knowing which structures can be used after them. We call the structures that occur after verbs **complements**. For reporting verbs, there are a number of different types of complements. Writers can use learner dictionaries and concordancers to help determine which structures can be used after particular verbs.

Table 10.2 shows different types of complement structures along with some of the reporting verbs with which they occur. Keep in mind that Table 10.2 does not show all the reporting verbs for each structure. Many reporting verbs can be followed by several different structures. For example, these verbs, among others, can occur either with a *that*-clause or a noun phrase after them: *acknowledge, advocate, confirm, deny, emphasize, indicate, mention, note, reveal, show.*

Table 10.2: Reporting Verbs and Complements

Verb + Noun Phrase		Examples
analyze	examine	This study analyzes *the effects* of sleep on concentration.
consider	focus on	This editorial compares *voters' reactions* to several proposals.
compare	identify	The authors distinguish *two types* of depression.
criticize	present	This article presents *arguments* in support of increased funding for
develop	provide	the arts.
discuss	refute	Table 5 summarizes *the results* of the analysis.
dismiss	reject	
distinguish	summarize	

Verb + *that*-Clause		Examples
advocate	find	The authors argue *that* adolescents have few safe alternatives to
argue	indicate	malls.
assert	imply	The study implies *that* self-evaluation is of value for students.
claim	maintain	The researchers conclude *that* more attention should be paid to the
comment	note	involvement of parents.
conclude	observe	These and other analyses predict *that* college fees may continue to
emphasize	predict	rise sharply.
explain	propose	

Verb + *wh*-Word Clause		Examples
consider	investigate	This article considers *why* the military did not intervene earlier.
describe	question	These findings question *whether* the intervention has been at all
discuss	wonder	successful.
examine		The researchers describe *which* methods were most successful.
identify		The authors discuss *how* the study of fish evolution is changing.

Verb+ *that*-Clause with *to*-Less Infinitive		Examples
advise	suggest	The results suggest *that* the government *monitor* offshore oil drilling
demand	urge	more carefully.
insist	warn	The researcher recommended *that* we *seek* better ways to identify
recommend		cases of child neglect.
		The author demands *that* dramatic steps *be taken* to reduce the
		budget deficit.

Verb + Indirect Object + *to* Infinitive Clause		Examples
advise	urge	This article advises *us to read* the fine print on loan applications.
caution	warn	The authors challenge *engineers to find* new solutions to this
challenge		problem.

Verb + *to* Infinitive Clause		Examples
fail		The author fails *to mention* one of the most important counter
neglect		arguments to her claim.
		The authors neglected *to point out* the limitations of their proposal.

Exercise 7

Use Table 10.2 to answer these questions.

1. Which structure seems to be most common after verbs that express an author's opinion? Why do you think that is the case?

   _____

   _____

   _____

2. Which structure tends to follow verbs that express what an author or piece of writing *does* with information (e.g., *analyzes*, *compares*) as contrasted to expressing the author's attitude or strength of a claim? Can you explain this tendency?

   _____

   _____

   _____

3. What observation can you make about the verbs that are followed only by a *to* infinitive clause?

   _____

   _____

   _____

Using Complements after Reporting Verbs of Advice

Using structures after reporting verbs that express advice can be especially challenging. As shown in Table 10.2, two types of complements can be used after some of these verbs. For example, with verbs like *advise, caution,* or *urge,* these are possible:

that + to-less infinitive

The author advises *that we be careful* in choosing an insurance policy.

indirect object + infinitive

The author advises *us to be careful* in choosing an insurance policy.

In most cases, the *to*-less infinitive will not look very different from other verbs other than third-person singular –*s* verbs, as in this example:

The author advises that we *consider* several options.

With two very common reporting verbs, *recommend* and *suggest,* only a *that*-clause or a noun phrase complement is possible, as in:

that + to-less infinitive

The author suggests   *that we be careful* in choosing the policy.

noun phrase

The author recommends $\left\{ \begin{array}{l} \textit{a careful look} \\ \textit{looking carefully} \end{array} \right\}$ at the policy.

The construction *suggest/recommend* + object pronoun + *to*-infinitive phrase is not grammatical. In other words, pronoun objects such as *me, her, us,* or *them* cannot be used before *to*-infinitive phrases with these verbs:

NOT: The author suggests/recommends us to be careful in choosing a policy.

Exercise 8

For each numbered item, circle two complements that can complete each sentence. The first one has been done for you as an example.

1. In the article "Can you hear me now?" Thomas Maugh II describes

    a. that the proportion of teenagers with hearing loss has increased during the last 15 years.

    (b.) increases in hearing loss among teenagers during the last 15 years.

    (c.) how hearing loss has increased among teenagers during the last 15 years.

2. A study, published in the *Journal of the American Medical Association*, reported

    a. that one in every five teens now has at least a slight hearing loss.

    b. slight hearing loss in one of every five teens.

    c. whether 20% of teens now have at least a slight hearing loss.

3. The researchers could not identify

    a. which specific cause was responsible for the increase in hearing loss.

    b. a specific cause for the increase in hearing loss.

    c. to be a specific cause for the increase in hearing loss.

4. However, many experts speculate

   a. that headphones used to listen to music may be a primary cause.

   b. headphones used to listen to music as a primary cause.

   c. whether headphones used to listen to music may be a primary cause.

5. They also found

   a. that some genetic differences accounted for hearing loss.

   b. genetic differences accounting for hearing loss.

   c. to be genetic differences that accounted for hearing loss.

6. In providing advice to teens, researchers recommended

   a. that they turn down the volume on MP3 players and wear ear protection at rock concerts.

   b. them to turn down the volume on MP3 players and wear ear protection at rock concerts.

   c. turning down the volume on MP3 players and wearing ear protection at rock concerts.

Exercise 9

Draw a line through the reporting verb that is inappropriate for the meaning or the structure in each sentence. Explain why the verb should not be used. The first one has been done for you as an example.

1. After a five-year review of the scientific literature concerned with corporal punishment of children, a task force concluded/ recommended/~~summarized~~ that parents should reduce or stop their use of physical punishment in disciplining children.

   Explanation: _The statement that follows the reporting verb is_
   a recommendation. The meaning of summarize does not fit this
   context; furthermore, summarize is rarely followed by a that-clause.

2. The task force, a group of experts in child development and psychology, determined/found/speculated that correlations existed between physical punishment and childhood anxiety and depression.

   Explanation: _____

   _____

   _____

   _____

3. Some studies also believed/observed/revealed correlations between physical punishment of children and aggression and impaired cognitive development.

   Explanation: _____

   _____

   _____

   _____

4. The task force was not, however, unanimous in the conclusions presented; some members of the task force contested/criticized/favored the evidence.

Explanation: _____

_____

_____

_____

5. One task force member who was not in agreement with the majority, Professor Robert E. Larzelere of Oklahoma State University, argued/contended/disputed that the evidence against spanking children was faulty.

Explanation: _____

_____

_____

_____

6. Larzelere cautioned/recommended/suggested that parents use spanking as a punishment if more gentle forms of punishment are unsuccessful.

Explanation: _____

_____

_____

_____

Appendix: Classifier Nouns

activity	constraint	forecast	program
accusation	course of action	framework	project
action	criterion (a)	goal	projection
advance	criticism	idea	purpose
advantage	decrease	illustration	question
advice	decline	improvement	reaction
aim	depiction	increase	reason
analysis(es)	description	information	requirement
application	development	innovation	representation
approach	difference	interpretation	research
argument	difficulty	issue	restriction
aspect	dilemma	item	result
assertion	disadvantage	limitation	scenario
assumption	disaster	link	shortfall
attempt	discovery	measure	situation
attitude	discussion	method	solution
background	disparity	mistake	stage
base/basis	distinction	motive	step
behavior	drawback	need	strategy
belief	effect	notion	study
catastrophe	effort	objective	subject
category	element	observation	suggestion
cause	episode	occurrence	system
challenge	event	outcome	task
change	evidence	outlook	technique
characteristic	example	phase	tendency
choice	expectation	phenomenon (a)	term
circumstance	experience	period	theory
claim	explanation	perspective	topic
class	facet	plan	tragedy
concept	fact	point	transition
concern	factor	possibility	trend
conclusion	feature	practice	type
connection	finding	problem	view
consequence	form	process	warning

Notes

Notes

Notes